The Tao of Tranquility

清靜經

The Tao of Tranquility

The Wisdom of Lao Tzu and the Buddha

Qingjing Jing

DEREK LIN

The Tao of Tranquility
The Wisdom of Lao Tzu and the Buddha – Qingjing Jing

2021 Paperback Edition, First Printing

Copyright © 2021 Derek Lin

ISBN: 979-8-53935-055-0 (Paperback)

Library of Congress Control Number: 2020915387
1. Qingjing Jing. 2. Lao Tzu. 3. Buddha. 4. Tao Te Ching. 5. Tao. I. Title.

Any references to historical events, real people, or real places are used fictitiously. Names, characters, and places are products of the author's imagination.

Cover art by Lin Hsin Chieh.
Book design by Lin Hsin Chieh.

Printed in the United States of America.

www.DerekLin.com

This book is dedicated to Master Wu Han-Yih (吳漢義).

I am grateful to Master Wu, not only for providing valuable guidance on the *Qingjing Jing*, but also for setting an example in cultivating the Tao over the years.

When it comes to Tao cultivation, Master Wu Han-Yih often emphasizes the importance of applying authentic teachings to daily life. In his view, knowing the ancient classics is not enough, if one cannot put that knowledge into action. His hope is that this book can be helpful to everyone, not only as a source of inspiration, but also as a guide for the practical application of the Tao.

Contents

The Tao of Tranquility

Introduction

This book you hold in your hands contains a most remarkable text from ancient China. It is called the *Qingjing Jing* (清靜經), pronounced like "ching jing jing" in Mandarin, where the second and third characters are different, and spoken with different tones — the fourth and first pitch respectively.

The *Qingjing Jing* was written about 1,250 years ago during the Tang Dynasty, by a Tao master who chose to remain anonymous. It occupies a halfway point in the history of the Tao, because the *Tao Te Ching* is roughly twice as old, predating us by about 2,500 years.

At the time of the Tang Dynasty, Buddhism had already spread throughout China. Some followers of Taoism and Buddhism saw the other side as a rival or the competition. Others, like the nameless author of the *Qingjing Jing*, saw an opportunity to bring the two great traditions together. Drawing from the best of Taoist and

Buddhist teachings, this master created a synergistic synthesis of spiritual power.

This extraordinary work quickly became popular and remained so throughout Chinese history. In every generation, students memorized the entire text, and scholars wrote extensive commentaries. Buddhists and Taoists alike regarded it as a significant work that combined the best of both worlds.

The *Qingjing Jing* is short. It contains under 400 Chinese characters, far less than the length of the *Tao Te Ching*. Its brevity comes from its tight focus on the foremost problem in spiritual cultivation: human suffering. The Buddha's solution to this problem was the Eightfold Path; Tao sages created their own solution by analyzing the problem at its most elementary level. The combination of the two is the central thesis of the *Qingjing Jing*.

The title of the *Qingjing Jing* can be translated as "Clarity and Tranquility Classic." The first character, *Qing* (清)

means pure, clean, and clear. In this title, it points specifically to the pure clarity of the spirit, which leads to clarity of mind and perception.

The second character, *Jing* (靜) means stillness, silence, and tranquility. In this title, it refers to the tranquil stillness of the spirit, when the noise of one's inner chatter has faded. Blessed silence prevails, so your soul can find peace, rest, and healing.

When we put these two characters together, we get *Qingjing* (清靜), meaning "clear tranquility" or "clarity and tranquility." This is the ultimate key to solving the puzzle of suffering. With this key, the mind beset with anxieties can finally settle down, so the spirit can open the door to peaceful enlightenment.

The third character, *Jing* (經) means a major work that is revered for its wisdom. It is the same character as "Ching" in *Tao Te Ching*, but written in the Pinyin romanization system instead of the older Wade-Giles system. Some translators render it as "Book," but that does not really convey its special status over regular books. *Jing* denotes a distillation of experience from previous generations that points out a path for future generations. Thus, rendering the character as "Classic" would be a much more accurate reflection of its original meaning.

The *Qingjing Jing* is indeed a classic, because it illuminates the most effective way to deal with the chaos of the material world. Do you sometimes feel like you have to rush around to put out one fire after another? If so, the *Qingjing Jing* will show you how to slow down and center yourself. When your mind finds peace, like disturbed water becoming still, it will regain its clarity.

You may not be familiar with this classic. You may not have heard of it before. Its lesson builds on Lao Tzu's original teachings of the Tao, so some of its passages are more profound. They can be harder to understand and translate, and perhaps that is why there are many books on the *Tao Te Ching*, but almost none on the *Qingjing Jing*.

Now, we have a great opportunity to explore this classic together. This special text from centuries ago is an advanced course on the Tao and Buddhist concepts that will take us to a higher level of spiritual refinement. Let us turn the page… and enter a whole new world.

* All *Tao Te Ching* translations quoted herein are from the author's original work published in 2006 as *Tao Te Ching: Annotated & Explained*.

清 靜 經

中英對照

Qingjing Jing

Original Text and Translation

Qingjing Jing

Verse 1

老君曰

大道無形
生育天地

大道無情
運行日月

大道無名
長養萬物

吾不知其名

強名曰道

Lao Jun says:

The great Tao has no form;
it gives birth to Heaven and Earth.

The great Tao has no emotions;
it moves the sun and moon.

The great Tao has no name;
it constantly nurtures all living
things.

I do not know its name;
I am forced to call it the Tao.

9

Qingjing Jing

Verse 2

That which is called the Tao:

夫道者

有清有濁   It has clarity; it has opacity.
　　　　　　　It has movement; it has tranquility.
有動有靜

天清地濁   The heaven is clear;
　　　　　　　the earth is opaque.
天動地靜   The heaven is moving;
　　　　　　　the earth is tranquil.
男清女濁

男動女靜   The male is clear;
　　　　　　　the female is opaque.
降本流末   The male is moving;
　　　　　　　the female is tranquil.
而生萬物

Descending from the source,
flowing into everything,
and giving birth to all living things.

清靜經

Qingjing Jing

Verse 3

清者濁之源

動者靜之基

人能常清靜

天地悉皆歸

夫人神好清

而心擾之

人心好靜

而慾牽之

The clear is the origin of the opaque; the movement is the foundation of tranquility.

If one can be constantly clear and tranquil, heaven and earth shall all return.

The human spirit prefers clarity, but the mind disturbs it.

The human mind prefers tranquility, but desires pull at it.

清靜經

Qingjing Jing

Verse 4

If one can constantly:

常能

遣其慾
而心自靜

dispel the desires, then the mind becomes tranquil by itself;

澄其心
而神自清

settle the mind, then the spirit becomes clear by itself.

自然六慾不生
三毒消滅
所以不能者

Naturally, the Six Desires will not arise, and the Three Poisons are eliminated.

為心未澄
慾未遣也

Thus, those who cannot do this, it is because their minds are not settled, and their desires have not been dispelled.

12

Qingjing Jing

Verse 5

能遣之者

內觀其心

心無其心

外觀其形

形無其形

遠觀其物

物無其物

三者既無

唯見於空

Those who can dispel desires:

observe their minds internally,
and there is no mind with their
minds;

observe their forms externally,
and there is no form with their
forms;

observe their things from afar,
and there is nothing with their
things.

Since these three are empty,
one can only see the emptiness.

13

Qingjing Jing

Verse 6

觀空亦空
空無所空

Observing emptiness is also empty; the emptiness has nothing to be empty.

所空既無
無無亦無

Since the emptiness has nothing, having nothing also has nothing.

無無既無
湛然常寂

Since having nothing has nothing, it is like water that is constantly still.

寂無所寂
慾豈能生

Since being still has no stillness, how can desires emerge?

慾既不生
即是真靜

Since desires do not emerge, this is true tranquility.

清靜經

Qingjing Jing

Verse 7

真常應物
真常得性
常應常靜
常清靜矣

The truly constant response to all things, is the truly constant attainment of nature.

Constantly responsive, constantly tranquil. This is constant clarity and tranquility!

Qingjing Jing

Verse 8

如此清靜
漸入真道

With such clarity and tranquility,
one gradually enters the true Tao.

既入真道
名為得道

Since one has entered the true Tao,
it is called attaining the Tao.

雖名得道
實無所得

Although it is called attaining the
Tao, in reality nothing has been
obtained.

為化眾生
名為得道

In order to transform sentient
beings, it is called attaining the Tao.

能悟之者
可傳聖道

Those who can realize this,
will be able to transmit the sacred
Tao to all.

Qingjing Jing

Verse 9

老君曰

Lao Jun says:

上士無爭

下士好爭

High-level individuals
do not contend;
low-level individuals
like to contend.

上德不德

下德執德

執著之者

不明道德

High virtue is not virtuous;
low virtue is attached to virtue.

Those who have attachments,
do not understand the Tao and
virtue.

Qingjing Jing

Verse 10

眾生所以
不得真道者
為有妄心
既有妄心
即驚其神
既驚其神
即著萬物
既著萬物
即生貪求
既生貪求
即是煩惱

The reason why sentient beings are unable to attain the true Tao, is because they have deluded minds.

Since they have deluded minds, they startle the spirit.

Since the spirit is startled, they become attached to myriad things.

Since they are attached to myriad things, they form covetous thoughts.

Since they form covetous thoughts, they become anxious.

Qingjing Jing

Verse 11

煩惱妄想
憂苦身心

Afflicted with anxieties and
delusions, worrying and suffering
in body and mind,

便遭濁辱
流浪生死
常沉苦海

often encountering murkiness and
disgrace, drifting aimlessly in birth
and death,

永失真道

constantly immersed in the ocean of
bitterness, forever losing the true
Tao.

清靜經

Qingjing Jing

Verse 12

真常之道
悟者自得
得悟道者
常清靜矣

The Tao that is true and constant:
those who realize it will attain it by
themselves;

those who realize and attain the
Tao, will possess constant clarity
and tranquility!

20

清 靜 經

註 釋

Qingjing Jing

Annotated & Explained

大道

Chapter 1: The Great Tao

Lao Jun says:

The great Tao has no form;
it gives birth to Heaven and Earth.

The great Tao has no emotions;
it moves the sun and moon.

The great Tao has no name;
it constantly nurtures all living things.

I do not know its name;
I am forced to call it the Tao.

"Lao Jun" is the highest title for Lao Tzu. At the time that the *Qingjing Jing* was written, the *Tao Te Ching* had been part of Chinese culture for centuries. Although "Lao Tzu" was already an honorific meaning "Old Master," it had become customary in religious Taoism to elevate it to "Lao Jun." This meant "Elder Lord," reflecting the belief that the wisdom of the Tao reigned supreme.

The first sentence of the *Qingjing Jing* says the Tao has no form, reiterating similar statements from the *Tao Te Ching*. This emphasis was particularly relevant in ancient times, when people had a strong tendency to personify the Tao and make a deity out of it. By stressing the formless first and foremost, Lao Tzu clarified that the Tao was not an entity with a face or body, and therefore could not be a mythological figure.

Today, the abstract nature of the Tao is something we can comprehend, due to our familiarity with science, physics and the myriad unseen forces of nature. In ancient times, it was a concept completely unlike the usual pantheons of deities that people expected. It was one of the ways that the Tao sages were ahead of their time.

This is why the Tao has always been depicted as an abstract symbol (the yin and yang or the bagua), and never as a god in paintings or sculptures. It is also why the Tao concept can be accepted by anyone from any faith, or a non-religious background.

Here, in the beginning of the *Qingjing Jing*, Lao Tzu points to the Tao as the formless source of creation. Giving birth to Heaven and Earth means creating the universe. Because the Tao is described as a void, this is equivalent to saying that the *somethingness* of the universe emerged from the *nothingness* of the Tao.

This is another point that ancient students of the Tao had to accept on faith. The Tao came with no creation myths. Lao Tzu never talked about *how* the universe was created. The world was not mixed together from primal elements by supernatural entities, nor was it brought into being through actions or commands by a creator. It came from nothing and out of nowhere. Ancient people might have regarded this as contrary to common sense.

Even today, some may still have trouble with this notion, because we feel more comfortable when we can associate a visible, tangible cause with an effect — like the parent of a child, or the hen that lays an egg. We may feel the assertion that all things emerge out of emptiness does not make sense, but it is essentially correct. Scientists hypothesize that the universe spontaneously came into existence about 14 billion years ago. This notion, based on theories and calculations, is not so different from what Lao Tzu and other Tao sages thought, based on intuition and reasoning.

To get a glimpse of their thought process, we only have to look at the everyday objects we use for various tasks. Where did they come from? Each one of them was invented by someone at some point in the past, but where was the idea for the invention before the inventor was born? When you really think about it, it seems the answer has to be... nowhere.

How about the ancestors of the inventor? You can identify the inventor's parents and grandparents. You can trace each generation back in time — but where was the previous generation before life appeared on Earth? Again, the answer is nowhere. No matter how you think about it, ultimately the source of everything is the nothingness of the Tao.

In the Tao framework, creation is not a construction process, but a birthing process. In that perspective, the universe is not the work of an architect who designed and built it for us. Rather, it is a miracle that came into being from the void, like a newborn emerging from the womb. Thus, if one had to assign a gender to the Tao, it would be feminine — the mother of everything — as opposed to the masculine God of Western culture.

The creation concept of the Tao applies to us too. We are not entities who just happen to inhabit this universe. We are an integrated part of everything. The molecules that make up our bodies come from the remnants of stars from eons past, like the molecules that make up everything else. A molecule that is part of a plant today could very well have been part of a human being long ago. We don't just live in the world — we are the world and the world is us. We all originate from the same source, and that makes us no less a miracle than the universe itself.

In the next sentence, Lao Tzu says the Tao has no emotions. This flows naturally from the understanding that the Tao is not a god, a mortal, or anything in between. Gods of mythology are often emotionally motivated, just like human beings. The Tao, on the other hand, acts without emotional motivation. We see its impartiality in the rain that falls on beautiful flowers and weeds alike. We also see it in the sunlight that shines on good and bad people with no preference. It does not favor one country over another in a war; it does not side with one team over another in a sports contest.

Indeed, the Tao does not resemble anything that we would normally associate with a deity. The Tao needs no fellowship with us, because it needs nothing beyond itself. It demands no worship from us, because it demands nothing from anyone. It experiences no joy when we follow it, and no sadness or anger when we turn away from it. We are the only ones who feel positive or negative emotions based on what we create for ourselves. Regardless of our feelings, the Tao offers no praise or condemnation, no approval or disapproval.

The Tao is the ultimate force behind all movements. Lao Tzu points to the sun and the moon as a way to reference all celestial bodies. At the cosmic level, the Tao governs the movements of all galaxies, stars and planets in the universe. At the planetary level, the Tao governs the movements of all living things in the Earth's biosphere. The Tao unifies all levels of existence, making everything part of this universal choreography, moving to the beat of a rhythm that we cannot hear — but can sometimes sense in a quiet moment.

To drive the point home, Lao Tzu closes his opening statement by noting that the Tao does not have a name. The countless gods of numerous pantheons all have names because humans create them as colorful, larger-than-life characters. The Tao is the opposite of that — it is the source that creates humans, not the other way around. It is something that had always existed, long before we came into being. It will continue to exist indefinitely, long after we are gone.

There is a certain kind of intelligence to the Tao. In the laws of nature, we see order and beauty. In nature itself, we see sophistication and intricacy. We may be tempted to think of the Tao as an intelligent designer — an entity that designs nature like we design our inventions. However, a closer look reveals the intelligence of the Tao is not at all like human intelligence. It does not function or communicate in any way similar to us, nor does it identify itself with a name like we do.

This concept is referenced several times in the *Tao Te Ching*. For instance, in chapter 25, Lao Tzu writes:

It can be regarded as the mother of the world
I do not know its name
Forced to identify it, I call it "Tao"
Forced to describe it, I call it great

"Great" is a fitting description, because we cannot deny its power. From the perspective of life, the Tao is the force in all living things to survive and thrive. It is also the fine tuning of the universe that allows for the possibility of life to manifest. It provides necessities like sunlight, air, water, gravity, and so on. Those who are ignorant may take such things for granted, while those who take the time to learn about them invariably feel humbled. The Tao is both the mother that gave birth to everything and a nurturing presence that cradles all. Without the Tao, we would not exist.

Although the Tao is nameless, human beings still need to call it something in order to talk about it. Out of all the possible names, the ancient sages were forced to call it "Tao," which was simply Chinese for "the path" or "the way." This is a fitting name, because we can say it

是the way of the universe and existence. Also, because we are all part of this totality, we can say it is the way of humanity. We use "Tao" as a label so we can study it, discuss it, and learn from it. All the while, we keep in mind that it is only a name — nothing more and nothing less.

The above depicts the Tao as the ultimate principle. It is more like natural laws than divine commandments. Our understanding of it is based on observations rather than revelations. We need not regard it as a deity, just like we do not regard physics or math as deities.

The Tao can be seen as a set of rules about how reality operates. When we don't understand the rules, they seem mysterious and random. When we do understand the rules, the mystery disappears, and we gain the ability to use them in a sensible way. This is why we study the *Qingjing Jing* — it provides the in-depth understanding that will empower us to attain mastery.

Questions for Reflection

1. If your name is only a label, then who are you?

2. What is your original nature, or your true self?

3. Are you aware of how something can come from nothing?

乾坤

Chapter 2: Yin and Yang

That which is called the Tao:

It has clarity; it has opacity.
It has movement; it has tranquility.

The heaven is clear; the earth is opaque.
The heaven is moving; the earth is tranquil.

The male is clear; the female is opaque.
The male is moving; the female is tranquil.

Descending from the source, flowing into everything,
and giving birth to all living things.

In this verse, Lao Tzu progresses from the One to the Two — from the unity of the Tao to the duality of yin and yang. This concept traces back thousands of years to the *I Ching*, where *qian* (乾) is the first hexagram symbolizing the male (yang), and *kun* (坤) is the second hexagram symbolizing the female (yin). Together, *qian kun* (乾坤) is the ancient Chinese expression for yin and yang.

The *Qingjing Jing* does not use these characters, but it definitely expresses the same meaning. There are two primary forces that manifest in every aspect of reality. These two forces are distinct, yet complementary to each other. They flow together and revolve around each other, giving rise to everything we see. This includes not only the living things arising from male and female energies, but also aspects of existence resulting from principles such as clarity and opacity.

When you study these complementary pairs, refrain from attaching value judgment to them. In the West, people may think in terms of light versus dark or good versus evil. In the authentic tradition of Tao wisdom, one has to let go of such notions. Yin and yang are not limited to simplistic descriptions, because they are not positive or negative in themselves. They can be beneficial when they are in balance, or harmful when they are out of balance. Therefore, we cannot align only with one side or the other, because we need to use both skillfully, guided by wisdom and moderation.

Movement and tranquility give us a good way to understand the above. Movement maps to the active yang state, while tranquility corresponds to the passive yin state. Either one can be harmful when taken to an extreme. When you have too much movement in your life, you end up with frantic rush and cannot catch your breath. When you have too much tranquility in your life, you end up with lethargic apathy and cannot motivate yourself. You need a mixture of both at the right balance for optimal results.

Heaven and earth form the first complementary pair to illustrate yin and yang. We can associate heaven with

清靜經

clarity (yang), and earth with opacity (yin). When we look to the sky, we can see clarity is the essence of heaven from the visibility of a sunny day, or the moon and the stars at night. When we look to the ground, we can see opacity is the essence of earth from the terrain around us, with all the rocks and soil that we cannot see through.

We can also see how heaven is associated with motion (yang), while the earth is associated with stillness (yin). During the day, the sun rises and sets. At night, the moon and stars gradually move across the sky. In contrast to this, the earth seems to be standing still. Its stillness gives us stable, solid ground, so we can have assured footing in a predictable environment.

As we explore these complementary pairs (clarity and opacity, movement and tranquility, heaven and earth), we also have to be aware that yin and yang are both sourced in the oneness of the Tao. If we lose sight of this and focus too much on the difference, we can create problems for ourselves. To resolve such problems, we

清靜經

need to get past the difference and connect with the unity behind the duality.

This concept can be rather abstract, but there is a story that illustrates the basic idea:

Once upon a time in ancient China, there was a monk traveling through the wilderness. He had walked the entire day, and it was getting too dark to keep going, so he looked around for a spot to rest. He found a few trees that looked safe, so he settled down as comfortably as he could. As daylight disappeared completely, he slept.

He woke up in the middle of the night, feeling extremely thirsty. It was so dark that he could not see anything, so he extended his hands to feel his way around. After a while, exploring in random directions, his hand touched something, and his fingers told him it was a bowl containing water. He marveled at his good luck. He drank deeply, enjoying the refreshing water as it quenched his thirst. He offered a prayer of gratitude to the Buddha for this blessing, and went back to sleep.

The next morning, the monk woke up. He looked around for the bowl from last night — and got the fright of his life. It wasn't a bowl at all. It was a dried-up, half-smashed skull, filled with rainwater. He looked inside it and saw insects crawling. He felt sick and nauseous.

Suddenly, it occurred to him that his feeling of sickness was not right. Everything was fine last night, but now it wasn't — why should that be? Now he had daylight, and last night he had darkness, but the water was the same. He felt good when he drank; it did not make him sick.

The only difference was his perception. It was his mind that was making him nauseous, not the water. Despite the difference of day and night, the water itself remained constant. His mind failed to get past the difference to see the sameness. He was the one who created the sharp distinction between what was drinkable, and what was not. It was illusory — and the cause of his problem!

As soon as he saw the reality of the situation, the sick feeling in his stomach vanished. He freed himself from the illusion, just by looking beyond the surface to perceive the underlying essence. What other troubles in life, he wondered, were illusions created entirely in his mind? How many problems did he cause himself needlessly in the past?

As we can see in this story, the monk's problem originated from his attachment to the difference between yin (the unseen) and yang (the seen). As soon as he let that go, the problem went away.

How can we apply this to life? Many of our society's issues are caused by too much attachment to differences — for instance, our differences in gender, age, race, religion, politics, and so on. It is only when we look past such differences that we perceive our essential unity, and realize we are all human beings originating from the same source. That realization creates the possibility for us to live in harmony.

This does not mean Tao cultivators ignore real differences in the real world. They acknowledge them without becoming attached to them. They make use of them by integrating them in synergistic ways. They can see this is how it works with nature, when yin and yang come together to create all living things.

In chapter 42 of the *Tao Te Ching*, Lao Tzu describes it as follows:

> *Tao produces one*
> *One produces two*
> *Two produce three*
> *Three produce myriad things*

"Two" in this context covers yin and yang, clarity and opacity, movement and tranquility, male and female. "Three" is change, or the dynamic interaction between the two. That interaction leads to myriad things, or all of creation.

This concept points to biological reproduction, but is not limited to it. As physical beings, we are part of nature, so we partake in the circle of life, just like all other living things. At the same time, we go well beyond that level. As sentient beings, we have the potential to transcend physicality, biology and procreation. That transcendence leads to the realm of spirituality and love. For us, it cannot be only about the mechanics of reproduction. Ultimately, love — the interplay of male and female energies — is the most essential of all.

This extra dimension means we have to elevate our thinking. Some people may equate yin and yang only with women and men, but we ought to know better than that. We should think of yin and yang not in terms of gender, but as energies that exist in everyone, *regardless of gender*.

Those who do not understand the above may resort to overly simplistic stereotypes. For instance, some may say men are transparent and action-oriented, while women are mysterious and passive. Their thinking does not match the real world, where it is not at all unusual for women to be active and dynamic (yang), and for men to be quiet and withdrawn (yin).

The last line of this verse returns to the theme of universal creation. It describes the Tao descending from the ultimate source, flowing into countless receptacles of life that are the myriad things of the world. This echoes Lao Tzu's words from chapter 1 of the *Tao Te Ching*:

> *The nameless is the origin of Heaven and Earth*
> *The named is the mother of myriad things*

The metaphor may vary — life flowing into containers like water, or life emerging from the birthing process — but the essence remains the same. The Tao is the power to give rise to all living things.

The above applies to you as well, because you are a microcosmic reflection of the Tao. Just as the unity of the Tao encompasses the duality of yin and yang, your being contains complementary energies. Just as the Tao integrates yin and yang to produce myriad things, you possess the ability to combine your energies to create manifestations in your life.

You are the co-creator of your reality. This is one of the most important concepts expressed in the *Qingjing Jing*. Hold on to it as you continue your exploration. Use it as you tap into your natural power of creativity, and create for yourself the life that you were meant to live.

Questions for Reflection

1. Do you have too much yin (apathetic passivity) in your life now?

2. Do you have too much yang (frantic activity) in your life now?

3. How can you integrate yin (thoughtful planning) and yang (determined actions) in your life?

Chapter 3: Human Beings

The clear is the origin of the opaque;
the movement is the foundation of tranquility.

If one can be constantly clear and tranquil,
heaven and earth shall all return.

The human spirit prefers clarity,
but the mind disturbs it.

The human mind prefers tranquility,
but desires pull at it.

Neither yin nor yang can exist by itself. Each half requires the other, like two sides of a coin. As depicted by the graceful curve in the yin-and-yang symbol, the two energies circle each other in an eternal dance. This is true everywhere we look, from the interactions of men (yang) and women (yin) to the transition from day (yang) into night (yin) and back again.

The yin-and-yang interaction of clarity and opacity follows the same pattern. To see this in action, we can look at a mountain stream. The water starts out crystal clear, perhaps from an underground source or melted snow. As it flows, it picks up dirt along the way. Gradually, the water becomes more and more opaque. The faster it moves, the more turbulent and muddy it gets. Thus, Lao Tzu describes the clear as the origin of the opaque.

Human nature also follows this pattern. We begin life with a pure essence, untainted by the material world. As we grow older, we become more cynical and lose the innocence of youth. As we encounter temptations, we chase after them and cause turbulence for ourselves. Like the mountain stream that starts out clear but picks up dirt along the way, our original clarity becomes increasingly unclear.

Imagine what happens when a fast-moving stream flows into a mountain lake. As it enters the larger body of water, it slows down and becomes one with the tranquil water. This transition from motion to stillness is why Lao Tzu says "the movement is the foundation of tranquility."

The correspondence of this concept with the *Tao Te Ching* can be seen in chapter 45:

> *Movement overcomes cold*
> *Stillness overcomes heat*
> *Clear quietness is the standard of the world*

It is a readily observed pattern in life, where movement brings about increased agitation, represented by heat. In order to cool down, one must slow down. After that, stillness makes it possible to reconnect with spirituality, and quietness makes it possible to regain tranquility.

This can be a metaphor for your personal encounter with the Tao. Visualize yourself as a turbulent current. Imagine what happens when you crash through the rapids, and suddenly arrive at a scenic and peaceful lake. It may be a bit of a surprise as you realize you can take it easy, relax, and connect with the beauty of nature. Gradually, the turbulence in you subsides, and the muddiness you've been carrying all along begins to settle. The confusion you've been feeling starts to fade. After a while, the water clears up completely. The tranquility of the lake has absorbed your chaos. You regain the clarity you had long ago, before you picked up all that dirt on your way to the lake.

This is a powerful experience, and if you can hold on to the clear and tranquil state, it is also transformative. The transformation in your life is described by Lao Tzu as heaven and earth returning to you, because tranquility and clarity reconnect human beings with the universe and all of existence. Thus, when you regain your original nature, you also regain everything that is worthwhile in your life.

The human spirit has a profound need for clarity. We gravitate towards it naturally, because it is the truest and purest essence of our original nature. This natural clarity is disturbed and distorted when the mind is bombarded by the sights and sounds of the material world. They are distractions that make it difficult for us to perceive anything clearly. They lure us into chasing one thing after another, only to end up empty-handed.

The human mind needs tranquility to function at its best. We all remember a time when the mental chatter quiets down, enabling total focus. We all know the mind can be extremely powerful and effective in such moments. We want more of the same, but the mind seems constantly disrupted by desires — mental noises that make the mind too busy to be tranquil.

Here, we should delve deeper into the very idea of

disruptive noise. We usually think of noise in terms of sound or cacophony. The Tao perspective goes further to note that the real culprit is not so much the noise, but the mind. If we possess true tranquility, then we can rest even when we are in a noisy environment. On the other hand, if we are attached to the issue of noise, then we will find no rest even when the environment is completely silent.

There is a story that can help explain this concept:

Once upon a time in ancient China, there was a young scholar who traveled to the imperial city for the civil service examination. He arrived months in advance, intending to spend the extra time in preparation. He knew that if he did well in the exam, his future would be assured.

He rented a room from an old man. Each day, after diligent study with friends, he would return to the room to sleep.

After a week, the old man came to speak with him: "Young man, I must tell you that my sleep has been disturbed ever since you moved in. Every night, when you return to your room, you kick off one shoe, and then the other. Each shoe makes such a loud noise that I am startled awake. Instead of kicking off your shoes, can you not take them off quietly?"

This complaint took the young scholar by surprise. He did not realize he had caused a problem. He apologized profusely, and promised to be much quieter.

The next night, he came back to his room late, as usual. He was so tired that he kicked off one shoe without thinking, out of habit. The sound it made reminded him that he needed to be much quieter. He removed his other shoe slowly, put it down lightly, and then tiptoed to his bed.

The next morning, the old man charged in. He said angrily: "That's it! I've had enough! You must move out!"

The young scholar said, "I am sorry, but was last night not an improvement? I remembered what you said after kicking off one shoe, so I took off the other one slowly. I reduced the noise by half!"

The old man glared at him: "Don't you understand? I waited for you to kick off the other shoe, so I could go back to sleep. I waited and waited, but the sound I was expecting never came, so I could not sleep the entire night! This is all your fault. You must move out!"

This story makes a good point: sometimes, it can be the lack of noise, rather than noise itself, that causes the problem. The old man's heart was full of resentment as he waited for the other shoe, so he had no peace even though there was no more noise that night.

This is why sages don't need to move far away from the city and live like a hermit. They know it's about the attachment in one's mind, rather than the noise of the crowds. The moment one becomes attached to the noise, one can be easily pulled off the peaceful path.

Desires have a similar impact in disrupting tranquility. The old man was not satisfied with what the young scholar felt was an improvement, because he still held on to the issue of noise. In a similar way, we will never be satisfied with material acquisitions, if we hold on to the attachment of desires.

Sometimes, we believe it is the lack of certain things that causes us to desire them. You may think: "I only want this one thing, and that's it. Once I have it, I'll be done." That one thing may be a new outfit, a new phone, or something else. You get your hands on it, only to realize it's not enough, and it's not the last thing. Satisfying a desire only stimulates more desires. The new outfit needs matching accessories, the new phone needs more apps, and so on. This becomes a never-ending cycle that makes tranquility impossible.

This may seem rather pessimistic, but Lao Tzu is only pointing out the obstacles to help you navigate through them, not to discourage you.

We have a natural preference for clarity and tranquility, but we are constantly pulled away by distractions and desires. When we understand these factors keeping us from the Tao, we can free ourselves from their influence.

If we continue our cultivation and apply the lessons, then we can be like the mountain stream entering the peaceful lake. We can regain our original nature that is clear and tranquil. Or, in the words of Lao Tzu — heaven and earth shall all return.

清靜經

Questions for Reflection

1. Are you able to slow yourself down when things get hectic?
2. Are you able to see things more clearly when you calm your mind?
3. Are you able to feel more tranquil when you manage and moderate your desires?

Chapter 4: Desires

If one can constantly:

dispel the desires,
then the mind becomes tranquil by itself;

settle the mind,
then the spirit becomes clear by itself.

Naturally, the Six Desires will not arise,
and the Three Poisons are eliminated.

Thus, those who cannot do this,
it is because their minds are not settled,
and their desires have not been dispelled.

At this point, we have learned that our overall problem is caused by the disrupting effect of excessive desires and mental chatter. Now we are ready to take a closer look at the Six Desires and the Three Poisons — terms that came from Buddhist teachings.

Lao Tzu never used these terms, because Buddhism was unknown in China back in his days. However, by the time the *Qingjing Jing* was written in the Tang Dynasty, Buddhism had gained widespread popularity. Many Buddhist terms had become part of the spiritual vocabulary, including the Six Desires and the Three Poisons.

The Six Desires are the specific ways you can be pulled away from your spiritual center. They are the cravings and urges associated with the following:

1. The Eyes — the desire to watch that which pleases the eyes, particularly beautiful sights such as luxurious objects or tempting treasures that can lead to avarice or lust.

2.   The Ears — the desire to hear that which pleases the
      ears, particularly flattering words and confirmation
      of one's preconceptions or prejudices.

3.   The Nose — the desire to smell that which pleases
      the nose, particularly heavy perfumes or cooking
      aroma that can stimulate yearning.

4.   The Tongue — the desire to taste that which pleases
      the tongue, particularly excessive food and drinks
      that can cause overindulgence and health issues.

5.   The Body — the desire to feel that which pleases the
      body, particularly physical comforts and sensory
      pleasures that can overshadow everything else.

6.   The Mind — the desire to think that which pleases
      the mind, particularly attachments and ego-centric
      delusions with little basis in reality.

Tao philosophy describes the above using different
words, but expressing the same essence. In chapter 12
of the *Tao Te Ching*, Lao Tzu writes:

The five colors make one blind in the eyes

The five sounds make one deaf in the ears

The five flavors make one tasteless in the mouth

Racing and hunting make one wild in the heart

Goods that are difficult to acquire

make one cause damage

Even with a cursory glance, one can see the similarities between Tao philosophy and Buddhist teachings. The Eyes correspond to the five colors, the Ears correspond to the five sounds, and the Tongue corresponds to the five flavors.

The Body is about the physical self in the material world, so it corresponds to racing and hunting — metaphors representing physical thrills. Similarly, the Mind is about attachments to material things, so it corresponds to goods — Lao Tzu's way of pointing to greed.

Whether we look at this from the Tao or Buddhist perspective, the common wisdom is that desires are detrimental to one's well-being. One may not realize this while one is under their spell, but when the spell is broken, one experiences a rude awakening.

Despite the damage desires can cause, we need not fear them, or expend a lot of effort to avoid them. There is no need to live far away from the sources of temptation. It is not so much about eliminating desires, but about recognizing desires as they occur, and dealing with them appropriately.

This is often easier said than done. Even the recognition can be tricky, because one can mistake desires as needs rather than wants. Also, more than one of the Six Desires can work together to lure you deeper into the trap, and that increases the difficulty in freeing yourself.

There is a story that highlights the nature of desires, and the challenges they bring into life. It is as follows:

Once upon a time in ancient China, there was a young man who had a dream of starting a business. He worked hard for years, and finally saved up enough money to set up his own store.

One day, while travelling on the road, he saw a small, delicately engraved box on the ground. Someone must have dropped it by accident.

Curious, he picked it up and opened it. Within was a pair of chopsticks intricately carved from ivory. Whoever owned them must be incredibly wealthy. The young man had never heard of anyone using chopsticks made of such precious material.

He waited by the road for a long time, but no one came back looking for the box. He decided to keep it for himself. Surely, he thought, this must be a blessing from Heaven!

When he got home, he could not wait to show off this find to his friends. He set the table, thinking about who to invite for dinner. Then, he noticed the ivory chopsticks next to his basic utensils — like rare gems next to crude pebbles.

He could not tolerate the mismatch. It was too glaring. He went out to purchase the finest silverware that could complement the ivory chopsticks better. They were expensive, so he had to dig into his savings.

He set his table again, and was satisfied that everything on the table looked better together. Then he frowned, noticing that his old table and chairs now seemed out of place.

He decided to buy all new, high-quality table and chairs that would be more suitable. This took more time, and required more money from his savings.

He set up the new table and chairs. As he expected, they complemented the ivory chopsticks and fine silverware nicely. Now the problem was the rest of his furniture in the house looked worn out and rustic. They had been that way for years, but he never noticed before.

He felt he had to replace all his furniture, to bring everything up to the new standard. This took even more time, and used up half his savings.

After much effort, he got everything in his house the way he wanted. Then, he saw there was still something not quite right. The house itself seemed too plain and rundown compared to all the new furniture in it.

He tried to ignore this, but it kept bothering him. Eventually, he decided a complete renovation was necessary. This took months, and wiped out all his savings.

At last, the renovation was completed. The house looked newer and more elegant than before, but now there was one more problem. The area outside the house was empty. He had nothing in his front yard.

He felt he had no choice but to have a garden built around his newly renovated house. This took many more months, and he had to borrow money to make ends meet.

By the time it was all finished, the whole process had taken more than a year. He went from having money saved up for his business to being deep in debt.

It all started when he found the small, delicately engraved box on the road. At the time, he thought it was a blessing from

Heaven. Now, he was not so sure. He reflected on everything he went through — and suddenly, he realized he never got around to inviting his friends... so he could show off the ivory chopsticks!

This story shows how desires can work their way into one's life. Initially, the young man had no awareness that he was ensnared by desires at all. At every stage of his downward spiral, he was certain the actions he took were necessary. He did not awaken from the delusion until he got to the end of his lesson.

Three of the Six Desires played a primary role in the lesson, and the first among them was the Eyes. To the young man, it was pleasing to see material things that "matched" at a similar level in terms of perceived value. He thought of this as an appreciation for aesthetics, but it was avarice, because what he acquired was beyond what he could actually afford.

The Ears played a significant role too. To the young man, it would be pleasing to hear his friends marvel at his find, express their envy, admire the beauty of the chopsticks, and congratulate him on his good fortune. The desire to hear such things provided the initial push that started the cycle of increasing expenditures.

The Mind was the factor behind both Eyes and Ears. This had to do with the young man's desire to think of himself as someone distinguished and successful. He wanted his friends to think of him in a similar way, and he assumed material things would make that happen. He ended up with the opposite. He was financially exhausted, and further from his dream of starting a business than before.

This sums up the danger of the Six Desires. When you chase after them, it is easy to lose yourself. You work against your own interests without realizing it. At the end of the chase, you catch only what you do not want — if you catch anything at all. By then, it may be too late.

Beyond the Six Desires, the *Qingjing Jing* also talks about the Three Poisons, which are the primary factors at the root of human misery. They can destroy your closest relationships and everything you have worked hard to build. They are the following:

1. Greed — this is a want that has been taken to an extreme. Greed gives rise to attachment, which escalates to fixation. It can blind you to everything in life as you single-mindedly go after your object of obsession. No matter how you try to satisfy the hunger, you cannot. Deep down, you know the pursuit is futile and ultimately empty, but you cannot give it up. It has locked you in.

2. Anger — this is the rage that originates from senseless fear. It starts as annoyance, but soon explodes into animosity and aggression. When you are gripped by anger, you attack those you think are responsible. It is a flame that feeds itself, so lashing out at others makes you more enraged, not less. You may vaguely sense this will lead to mistakes you

will regret later, but you are powerless to stop
yourself.

3. Ignorance — this is the confusion brought about by
    the lack of awareness and learning. It may also be a
    self-inflicted condition, if one stubbornly ignores
    contrary evidence and sticks to dogmatic beliefs.
    Those who are poisoned by ignorance cling to
    wrong ideas leading to wrong decisions, refusing to
    learn anything new, even when it is obvious that
    they are headed in the wrong direction.

Three Poisons are formidable challenges. They are not
temporary, so they will not go away on their own. They
are not simple, so they cannot be solved with common
self-improvement techniques. The best way to solve
them lies in the proper handling of desires.

While some spiritual teachers say we need to eliminate
desires, Tao sages say we should dispel them. Desires
are a natural part of life, and all living things have them.
Animals have the desire to continue living, and human

beings have even more elaborate desires that go beyond basic survival. Desires will always be around, so there can be no true elimination of them. The better way is to dispel the desires that are not necessary or useful, so we can be more focused and less distracted.

The process of dispelling desires and settling the mind is much like letting an agitated pool of water become still. Initially, desires are like pebbles dropped into the pool. They form ripples and cause distortions on the pool's surface reflection. The wrong way to get rid of the ripples is by sweeping a hand over the surface in an attempt to smooth them out. The more this is done, the more ripples are created — because suppressing desires only serves to strengthen them.

When you dispel desires, you stop dropping pebbles into the pool. When you release attachments, you stop trying to smooth the ripples with your hand. You allow the ripples to go away on their own, without any interference from you. It may be difficult at first, when you feel the urge to *do something*. That is the effect of an action-oriented mindset, and once you realize it, you can simply let it go.

After a while, the surface of the pond will become glassy smooth. In the clarity of its reflection, you can see the truth about the Six Desires and the Three Poisons. Like the ripples that are no longer present, they have gone away naturally, and can no longer trouble you.

These steps outlined by the sages are simple, but not necessarily easy. Not everyone can follow them to arrive at the end result of clarity and tranquility. Those who cannot will continue to live in the agitated state. Stirred up by desires, they cannot keep themselves from interfering with the mind's natural preference for peace. As long as this is the case, they will remain victims of the Six Desires and the Three Poisons.

Now we can see the importance of this verse. It helps us analyze the different desires, and warns us about the potential poisons. We gain insights about their causes and symptoms, as well as effective treatments and remedies. This is the essential lesson that will ultimately enable us to dispel desires and neutralize poisons in our lives.

Questions for Reflection

1. What is the difference between eliminating desires and dispelling desires?

2. Can you identify the elements of the Six Desires that are present in your life?

3. How can you best handle the Three Poisons that can be harmful for your spirituality?

觀

Chapter 5: The Observation

Those who can dispel desires:

observe their minds internally,
and there is no mind with their minds;

observe their forms externally,
and there is no form with their forms;

observe their things from afar,
and there is nothing with their things.

Since these three are empty,
one can only see the emptiness

Starting with this verse, the *Qingjing Jing* focuses on the methods that will help us become clearer and more tranquil. These methods begin with *guan* (觀), which means the observation of everything from a detached and objective perspective.

To do this properly, it is necessary to dispel desires first, as detailed in the previous chapter. This is a necessary step, because desires have an obscuring effect, like clouds blocking the moon at night. People trapped in desires are spiritually in the dark. They cannot see much around them, so they look at only what they want to see and confirm only what they already believe. They convince themselves they are right while heading down the wrong path, like traveling at night without the moonlight to guide them.

If you dispel desires before making observations, then it is as if the dark clouds have parted to reveal the bright moon. You see things as they are, not as you wish them to be. You are free from attachments, so you can observe without preconceptions. The illumination enables you to follow the evidence wherever it leads — even in an unexpected direction, which can give you new insights.

The practice of observation begins with introspection. This is like modern machinery running diagnostics when starting up. If it passes the self-test, then it can report functional readiness.

When you look within, you are likely to find your mind in a fluctuating state of constant change. You may have a lot of internal chatter. You may also find internal commentaries on the chatter, and even commentaries on the commentaries. For example, suppose you find yourself thinking, "I wonder what people say about me?" Then, you ask yourself: "Should I care what they say?" Finally, you tell yourself: "I am worrying about this too much. I need to stop." Such thoughts buzz through the mind, piling on one another randomly. There seems to be no end to them.

As distracting as the internal chatter can be, all your thoughts are ultimately transient, and the emotions they carry are also transient. You can see how your emotions come and go when you place them under observation. None of them has any permanence, not even strong, negative emotions like sadness or anger. Although they seem powerful, it is entirely possible for you to discard them whenever you want, merely by directing your attention somewhere else.

As an emotion goes away, whatever power it has over you vanishes as well. This simple concept can be the first step for you to assert control. Being able to master emotions means you are no longer at their mercy, and you can use them skillfully in your own best interests. You are in charge; your mind must obey your command and do what you tell it to do, for it does not have a mind of its own. Or, as the *Qingjing Jing* says, there is no mind with your mind.

In the study of Buddhism and Taoism, you will find even more depth and details in the analysis of the mind. For instance, there is an often-told story about the *Diamond Sutra* that provides further insights:

About twelve hundred years ago, there lived a notable Zen master by the name of Deshan. For years, he studied the Diamond Sutra, wrote volumes of commentaries, and became widely praised for his knowledge.

One day, he heard about a new doctrine on the sudden realization of Buddhahood. It was taught by Zen monks in southern China who advocated the possibility of becoming enlightened by pointing directly to the mind.

This struck Deshan as completely wrong. He felt a need to confront them, debate them, and destroy their false beliefs. He packed up all of his Diamond Sutra commentaries and started on the long road heading south.

After much travel, Deshan came across a small teahouse where an old woman sold rice cakes. He was hungry, so he approached her: "I would like to buy some rice cakes. How much are they?"

Instead of answering, the old woman became curious about the baggage he was carrying. She pointed to it and asked:

"That looks very heavy. What's in it?"

Deshan could not keep the pride out of his voice as he set his baggage down: "The commentaries I have written on the Diamond Sutra."

"How interesting!" the old woman exclaimed. "I happen to have a question about the Diamond Sutra. If you can answer it, I will gladly give you the rice cakes for free. If you cannot, then I'm afraid I cannot sell you any rice cakes."

Deshan was a bit surprised by this, but did not see it as much of a challenge. Who knew more about the Diamond Sutra than he did? What could anyone, especially an old woman in a backward rural area, ask him to really test his knowledge? With confidence, he nodded: "Go ahead, ask your question."

The old woman said: "It is written in the Diamond Sutra that 'the past mind cannot be obtained, the present mind cannot be obtained, and the future mind cannot be obtained.' So tell me, when you wanted to buy my rice cakes just now, with which mind were you thinking?"

Deshan was dumbstruck. With which mind indeed? He could think of no possible answer to give. The old woman quoted the Diamond Sutra perfectly and caught him in a trap from which there was no escape. In that moment, he had the sudden realization that the knowledge he thought he possessed, the knowledge others praised... was nothing more than his own ego deluding him.

Deshan knew he had to leave. In defeat, he picked up his baggage to get on his way. The commentaries that made him so proud just a moment ago... now seemed totally inadequate. He still had much to learn before mastering the teachings of the Diamond Sutra.

As this story illustrates, the *Diamond Sutra* goes even deeper into the concept that there is no mind with your mind. You cannot obtain your mind of the past, because the past is already gone. You cannot go back in time to unmake your mistakes, or unthink the thoughts you already had.

You cannot obtain your mind of the present, because the

present moment does not stay still. Trying to hold on to it is like trying to hold on to the water of a flowing stream. The present is constantly shifting, transforming itself into the past with every instant. There is nothing you can do to hold on to it.

It is every bit as impossible to obtain the mind of the future, because no one can predict the future perfectly. You can try to guess what you will think at some point down the road, but when that moment comes, your mind may already be onto something else. The situation you anticipated has changed, possibly beyond all recognition. Thus, attempting to obtain your future mind can only be futile.

Having observed yourself mentally, you can turn your gaze outward to observe yourself physically. The human body seems to be the same from one moment to the next, but that is illusory. You are getting a bit older every moment, whether you realize it or not. As you go through this aging process, your body will change, positively or negatively.

When it comes to fitness, you can get stronger if you engage in physical activities — or weaker if you neglect exercise for too long. When you get sick, you can get better if you seek medical help — or worse if you ignore your symptoms. It is a certainty that you will change physically no matter what. Indeed, you are changing in small ways even now, as you read these words.

The conclusion is inevitable: no one has a fixed form. Everyone is subject under the same continuous change as everyone else. A few people seem able to delay aging and maintain youthful appearance longer than the rest, but eventually they must also yield to the passage of time.

In this regard, the situation today has not changed fundamentally from ancient times. Although science has lengthened life expectancy, our existence is still ephemeral. We may wish to continue living as we are now, but there is nothing for us to grasp onto, because nothing about human beings lasts forever. In the words of the *Qingjing Jing*, there is no form with our forms.

This overall impermanence you observe in the mind and body applies to everything else, and the *Qingjing Jing* specifically points to "things" as the next example. In the context of the world, this is a reference to the myriad things. The central and fundamental idea in the Tao is that nothing lasts; everything in the world comes and goes. The myriad things have no lasting reality — just like you and me.

In the context of your little corner of the world, this is a reference to all the material things in your life. Look at the objects around you. They can last longer than we do, but they are also not eternal. Consider a family heirloom that has been passed down through the generations. It may outlast individual family members by many decades, but it too can be destroyed at any time and cease to exist.

Consider the great outdoors. Initially, the landscape may seem permanent, but that too is an illusion, because it is constantly eroded by nature. It can also change instantly, in catastrophic events such as earthquakes or

清靜經

volcanic eruptions.

Those who have studied Buddhist philosophy will find this concept familiar. The Buddha taught that the world was illusory because all things were transient. This teaching is timeless. It is just as true for us today as it was to the Buddha and his disciples long ago.

Sometimes, impermanence can be surprising. When we look at houses, buildings, and other constructions, we may feel that they will remain as they are. One day, something has changed — perhaps a warehouse has been demolished, or a store has gone out of business, or a meadow has been paved over and is now a parking lot. We may be surprised, even though intellectually we know nothing lasts. It is exactly as the *Qingjing Jing* tells us — there is nothing with our things.

The first chapter of the *Tao Te Ching* says:

> *Thus, constantly without desire,*
> *one observes its essence*

Constantly with desire,

one observes its manifestations

This means our observations can be misleading in the desiring state, but the truth becomes evident in the desireless state. Without the interference of desires, we perceive emptiness as the essence of existence. Whether we look at ourselves or the world, we can find no permanence anywhere.

This is why the mind, the form, and all things are empty. It is no wonder that people end up empty-handed when they become fixated with book knowledge, youthful appearance, or material possessions. Beyond the basics of life, the pursuit of empty things will only get you more emptiness.

In this limitless void, there is only the eternal Tao. It stands alone like a lighthouse, a beacon of constant truth in a world of endless change, providing everlasting illumination in the deepest darkness. While everything comes and goes, flickering in and out of existence, the

Tao remains. It is the one real thing in an unreal world — and that is exactly what makes Tao cultivation the most worthwhile and meaningful endeavor of all.

Questions for Reflection

1. Have you taken the time to observe your mind internally?

2. Have you taken the time to observe your physical self externally?

3. Have you taken the time to observe the world from an objective perspective?

Chapter 6: Emptiness

Observing emptiness is also empty;
the emptiness has nothing to be empty.

Since the emptiness has nothing,
having nothing also has nothing.

Since having nothing has nothing,
it is like water that is constantly still.

Since being still has no stillness,
how can desires emerge?

Since desires do not emerge,
this is true tranquility.

This verse can be difficult to understand, even for those who are able to read ancient Chinese. The difficulty comes not from the language, but from the concepts presented. When Chinese commentators attempt to explain, they are not always successful. When Western scholars attempt to translate, the difficulty multiplies. This may be one of the reasons why the *Qingjing Jing* is relatively unknown in the West.

Let us take a closer look at the concepts. Once they are properly analyzed, you will see they make perfect sense. We can begin the analysis by building on the paradigm of emptiness as discussed in the previous chapter.

The emptiness of the Tao is unlike the conventional concept of emptiness, because it is not a vacuum or an unchanging state of nothingness. It seems like a void, but it is filled with unlimited potentialities which will take on physical reality when the time is right. It is an active, dynamic emptiness, and the source of universal creation discussed in previous chapters.

As a human being, you are connected to the Tao at a fundamental level, so the power of creation is in you too. It manifests as your creativity, and you see it at work every time you come up with ideas. These ideas seem to emerge out of nowhere, and the ones you act on will manifest in your world. The process goes from nothingness (no ideas at all) to the intangible (an idea) to the tangible (a real-world result). This is how the Tao functions throughout existence, from cosmic creation starting with the Big Bang at the universal level, to all our inventions and artistic works at the personal level.

Observe the void in the core of your being. This act of observation is your consciousness turning inward upon itself. The essence of emptiness in you is observing, and also being observed. The emptiness you contemplate internally is the same consciousness that is doing the contemplation. In other words, it is a process of the emptiness (your mind) watching the emptiness (itself).

That's not all. To understand the void and become one with it, you must completely blank out your mind and discard all thoughts. Then, you must elevate your thinking to the next level, and blank out even the whole idea of blanking and discarding. Continue until there is nothing left — including the very idea of "nothing" — even that should disappear completely without a trace.

If this seems like a paradox, rest assured that the Tao is not supposed to be a riddle wrapped in a mystery inside an enigma. That may be the media stereotype of the Tao, but the authentic Tao is much more simplistic and practical. The following steps may help you get a handle on it:

- Let go of all your thoughts, and then let go of the concept of letting go.
- Empty out your mind, and then empty out the thought of emptying your mind.
- Clear out everything in your mind, and then clear out the process of clearing out everything in your mind.

This verse is the most crucial, most valuable, and most

清靜經

mind-bending part of the *Qingjing Jing*. If you are able to digest and absorb what it means — the recursive process to let go of letting go — then you will obtain a precious piece of the puzzle known as Enlightenment.

When the ancient sages taught this lesson, they were not trying to confuse anyone. They were trying to describe something very basic in a simple way. It is, in fact, so basic that we experience it all the time without thinking about it. We can leverage that experience to deal with it from a practical angle.

Imagine it is now your bedtime. You are trying to fall asleep. You anticipate being busy tomorrow, so you know you have to get quality sleep tonight. You tell yourself to fall asleep as quickly as possible. You tell yourself to stop thinking so you can rest.

After a while, you find yourself still awake. You cannot fall asleep, because you keep telling yourself to fall asleep. You cannot stop thinking, because you keep telling yourself to stop thinking. The process of stopping requires thinking, so you have created a perfect trap, and you cannot get out of it.

You try harder, but that turns out to be a mistake. The harder you try to fall asleep, the harder it gets. The more willpower you exert on yourself, the farther you push the goal away. After a while, you have to admit that increasing efforts only turn into increasing resistance. This is a sign that you are moving against the Tao, not with it.

At this point, there are two possible scenarios. In the negative scenario, you begin to worry. What if I cannot fall asleep tonight? What if I am too tired tomorrow morning, when I need to be at my best? What if my fatigue causes me to fail? How will that impact me? Why is it so difficult to fall asleep? Before long, your worry turns into anxiety and even panic. Perhaps you turn to sleeping pills out of desperation.

In the positive scenario, you recall the lesson from the Tao, and begin to understand where you went wrong.

Your mind is like a computer that keeps executing the "stop" instruction. It cannot stop because it is too busy processing the instruction. The thought "I will stop thinking right now" is the ironclad guarantee *against itself*. What you must do instead is turn off the mental computer and let go of all mental activities. Only then will you be able to relax, and get the sleep you need.

The same idea applies to everything, not just sleep. There is a story that drives home this point, to make it especially memorable:

Once upon a time in ancient China, there was an alchemist of a mystical Tao lineage known for incredible feats and supernatural powers. One day, he came to a village where the men worked backbreaking jobs at a nearby gold mine. He told them they didn't have to work so hard. There was a better way to make a living.

The villagers were surprised to hear this. They all said: "Master, what is this better way? Please tell us!"

The alchemist agreed to help. "I will show you," he said.

He instructed them to fill a pot with water and sand from a nearby river. "Notice the sand contains tiny gold specks in it, because the water of the river flows from the general direction of the gold mine," the alchemist said. "I have now imbued this pot with divine alchemical powers, so all you have to do is stir the water and sand while concentrating the mind. Light a small candle before you start stirring. By the time the candle burns out, you'll see many gold nuggets at the bottom of the pot. Isn't this much easier and faster than digging for gold in the mines?"

The villagers could not believe such a thing was possible, so the alchemist demonstrated for them to prove it. Sure enough — when the stirring was done, they all stared incredulously at gold nuggets produced in this miraculous way.

"My work here is done," the alchemist said. He got ready to leave, but the villagers weren't ready to let him go.

"Master, please wait!" They pulled at his sleeves. "You said

we have to stir while concentrating the mind. Can you be a little more specific on how we should do that?"

"Oh, it's simple." The alchemist assured them. "There is only one rule to follow: while stirring the pot, you must never, ever think any distracting thoughts. The moment you are distracted, even for the briefest instant, the alchemy will fail and the gold nuggets will not appear."

The villagers were a little puzzled. They said: "Distracting thoughts? Master, can you give us an example?"

The alchemist said: "Anything can be a distracting thought, like the monkey in the tree for instance."

The villagers thought they understood, so they thanked the alchemist profusely. He wished them luck, and went on his way.

Excitedly, the villagers tried to create gold for themselves. They fetched more water and sand from the river to fill the pot. Then, they assigned a strong young man to do the stirring. As they were lighting the candle to start the process, they reminded him: "Remember, no monkey in the tree!"

It didn't work. The young man could not keep the monkey out of his mind before the candle burned out. No gold nuggets appeared, and everyone was disappointed.

Another villager stepped forward. He closed his eyes, steadied his mind, and then started stirring. For a moment, it seemed as if he might succeed, but then he began to waver. He struggled with it, taking deep breaths. After a while, the strain of concentration was too much. He lost control, thought of the monkey, and failed.

One by one, all the villagers tried their hands at stirring the pot. None of them could resist thinking of the monkey. The harder they commanded themselves to not think the thought, the more quickly they were defeated.

After weeks of effort, they were all exhausted. They had to admit that the monkey was just too crafty. No matter how they tried to keep it out of the mind, it would find its way in somehow. The instruction from the alchemist might be simple, but it was far from easy. Reluctantly, the men of the village returned to their old jobs at the mine.

This story highlights the inherent difficulty in managing the mind with the force of the mind. Stirring for gold is like willing yourself to go to sleep. The more mental power you bring to bear, the more you guarantee your own failure. This is a theme that runs through numerous Tao teachings. Being forceful and aggressive is the strategy many people use for most things in life, but oftentimes it is the worst way to go.

The monkey in the story represents a mental state you do not want, and yet cannot control. Remaining awake when you need to sleep is one example, but there are many others. It is also a reference to a central Buddhist teaching that compares the cravings of the human mind to a monkey. Such cravings make people chase one thing after another, like a monkey leaping from tree to tree, grasping one vine after another.

Whether from the Buddha or the Tao, the teaching is clear: do not try to suppress the monkey, because that will only make things worse. Do not try to banish the monkey, because it will find a way back into your mind. That which you resist will persist, so the best way to deal with the monkey is to tame it — and the only way to tame it is through clarity and tranquility.

That's all there is to it. *Qingjing*, the state of clarity and tranquility, means you don't just stop thinking — you must also stop thinking about stopping. Your mind becomes like the void of the Tao. This brings the monkey under control which, in our sleeping example, means you can finally get some rest.

It's a bit ironic, because sleep is the most natural thing imaginable. Billions of human beings drift off to sleep every night. How does something like this, which started out being so easy and simple, become difficult or even impossible?

Thinking is the key. The thinking mind is a powerful

tool. We use it all the time, but it is only a tool, so it can be misused or overused. When this tool gets in the way of you following the Tao, using it more will only turn it into a bigger obstacle. Thinking about material things invariably gives rise to desires — and increasing desires take you away from the state of true tranquility.

To get back on track with the Tao, you need to reverse course. When you need to sleep, rest or meditate, throttle back the thinking in your mind. Whatever thoughts appear, let them disappear on their own without any attempt to grasp onto them. Use your rational faculties less and less, and then stop using it altogether.

To fully express this concept, the *Qingjing Jing* uses the term *zhan ran* (湛然), originally derived from water that is deep, perfectly still, and completely clear. It describes a mental state that is undisturbed, unmoved, and absolutely peaceful.

You can apply this term for yourself. Let your mind be

like a deep pool of water. Let the stray thoughts fade, and let any disturbance dissipate. Soon, the only thing that remains will be the crystal clarity that comes with the ultimate stillness.

In this stillness, nothing stirs — not even the concept of stillness. In this profound silence, you hear nothing — not even the sound of silence. It is a tranquility where desires cannot emerge, for there is nothing to desire, and there is no desiring of desires.

This is the *emptiness of emptiness*. Or, as Lao Tzu says in chapter 37 of the *Tao Te Ching*:

> *Without desire, using stillness*
> *The world shall steady itself*

This is a penetrating insight that gets right to the point. In the simplicity of the nameless, there is nothing to disturb anything, and even the concept of nothingness is completely absent. This *nothingness of nothingness…* is the ultimate meaning of true tranquility!

Questions for Reflection

1. Can you empty your mind?

2. Can you empty the emptiness in your mind?

3. Can you settle your mind, like water becoming still?

常應

Chapter 7: Constant Response

The truly constant response to all things,
Is the truly constant attainment of nature.

Constantly responsive, constantly tranquil.
This is constant clarity and tranquility!

清靜經

Clarity and tranquility are not static states. They can be influenced and disturbed by external factors. Thus, the work of spiritual cultivation is not done when we master the art of emptying the emptiness. We still must know how to keep ourselves in the quiet stillness.

Think of what happens when you are deeply immersed in meditation, and a noise pulls you out of it. This is disruptive, because you have to remain for a while in the meditative state to benefit from it. The same is true for cultivation. You may be able to apply the Tao and reach equilibrium, but that alone is not enough. Life is constantly changing, so something may happen at any time to knock you off balance. What would be the best way to prepare for this, so you can maintain your peace of mind?

The one certainty about change is that we know it absolutely, positively will occur. The only thing that never changes is change itself. That's why it occupies such a central place in Tao teachings. *I Ching*, the earliest book on the Tao, can be translated as the *Classic of*

Changes, because it is all about the patterns of change in life. It predates the *Tao Te Ching* by more than two thousand years, and it is the work of ancient masters revered by Lao Tzu.

Knowing that change is inevitable, you can see the wisdom of watching for it. The anticipation lets you respond right away when change occurs. Like a tightrope walker, you can apply constant adjustments in an unstable environment to avoid falling. You maintain dynamic balance as you stay upright and continue moving forward.

This is the art of constant response from the *Qingjing Jing*, and it requires mindful awareness. It means being aware of the feelings within you and the forces around you. All the factors at play, internal and external, visible and invisible, are constantly shifting and affecting one another.

Even more important than the above is the detached observation from chapter 5. At any given moment, you need to know not only what is happening, but also the reason behind it. Why are you engaged in a particular activity? Does it really make sense?

The above can be a rather subtle point, so it would be best for us to illustrate it with a story, as follows:

One day, a Tao sage was traveling through the wilderness, and noticed a commotion up ahead. When he got closer, he saw two men engaged in a heated argument. They seemed really worked up over something, so the sage approached.

Both men were hunters, and they were arguing over numbers. One of them said if you caught eight animals every day for three days, you would end up with twenty-four. The other disagreed, and said the answer should be twenty-three. Each of them was sure the other was wrong. Neither was willing to back down.

Their argument was going nowhere, so they decided arbitration was the only way. They asked the sage to render a decision to settle their dispute, and the winner would take the loser's hunted game for the day.

They each explained their views, and the sage listened patiently. When both sides were done, the sage rendered his verdict. He pointed to the hunter who said twenty-three: "You are right. You may take what your friend has hunted today."

The winning hunter grinned. He took his prize and went on his way, looking satisfied and smug. The hunter who lost was shocked beyond words. He could not go against the decision, since he had already sworn to be bound by arbitration, but he was outraged.

He turned to the sage in frustration: "Adding up eight three times gets you twenty-four! This is so simple that even children understand it. You seem to be a wise man. How can you not know such an obvious thing?"

The sage smiled: "Of course you are correct. Of course the true answer is twenty-four. Of course it is obvious. Now, think about what you are doing. If someone cannot even comprehend such a simple thing, then what is the point to argue with him?"

The hunter was stunned. He was so caught up in the argument that he never paused to think about the situation.

The sage continued: "That hunter thinks he has won. He has the prize today, but he also has delusional beliefs — not just for today, but probably for his entire life. You think you have lost, but you have actually gained a valuable lesson."

The hunter realized the truth in the sage's words. To argue with a fool means being even more foolish than the fool. Did he really want that? Why waste precious time, when life was already too short?

The wisdom of the sage in this story is something we can all apply for ourselves. All too often, we see people expressing views that are obviously wrong, so we cannot resist the temptation to debate them. We want to set them straight, without realizing that we may be lowering ourselves to their level for no particularly good reason. We may know what's going on and what we want to do, but we are not thinking about the reasons why we should or should not do it. Thus, our response to the situation may not be the best. It may not be in accordance with the Tao.

This does not mean we always avoid getting involved. The Tao is not just about doing nothing or going with the flow. Your involvement in the various events of life, like the yin and yang symbol, must have a dynamic side to complement the mindful side.

Living the Tao is not like laying back in a canoe, and letting the river carry you anywhere. In that paradigm, your peace can be easily disrupted when the canoe runs into an obstacle.

Living the Tao is more like being on a surfboard, and skillfully riding a giant wave. Sometimes, this means going along with the force of the wave. Other times, it means adjusting yourself according to the situation. In that paradigm, you can be active while the mind remains perfectly at peace.

Once you understand this concept, it will be easy for you to spot those who do not. They are the ones who refuse to make any adjustments for the world, but insist that the world should make adjustments for them. They may say "I'm just the way I am," or "I've got to be me," or "Why should I change for anyone?"

People who think that way may believe they have certain characteristics that are set in stone. They may not know that physically, millions of cells are replaced in the human body every day. Mentally, everyone is constantly learning new ideas and discarding old ones. After a while, you are literally walking around in a new body and with a new mind. There is no question you have changed, you are changing right now, and you will continue to change.

The only question, then, is *how* you will change in response to all things. Will you change according to the dictates of trends, fads, and society's expectations? Or, will you take charge to direct your own physical, mental and spiritual evolution? In this verse, Lao Tzu is pointing out that you have a responsibility to respond. What should your response be?

The best response of all is using the Tao externally and internally. When you use the Tao in dealing with the world, you are constantly responsive to everything as it happens, like a clear mirror providing an undistorted reflection for all changes as they occur. This is what Lao Tzu means by "the truly constant response to all things."

You wield the Tao in your thoughts as well. This means self-honesty and self-discipline. When you fail to live up to your own expectations, you make no excuses. When you veer off from a plan you set, you get back on track. Your self-reflection reveals your original nature, which in turn reflects the Tao. This is what Lao Tzu means by "the truly constant attainment of nature."

When you bring the external response and the internal attainment together, you will be ready to open the next door. Beyond the door is true tranquility — the path that will get you closer to the Tao than ever before!

Questions for Reflection

1. How will you use the constant Tao to respond to
    all things?
2. How will you use the constant Tao to attain your
    true nature?
3. How will you maintain constant tranquility in
    daily life?

得道

Chapter 8: Attaining the Tao

With such clarity and tranquility,
one gradually enters the true Tao.

Since one has entered the true Tao,
it is called attaining the Tao.

Although it is called attaining the Tao,
in reality nothing has been obtained.

In order to transform sentient beings,
it is called attaining the Tao.

Those who can realize this,
will be able to transmit the sacred Tao to all.

This verse is a milestone. Everything prior to this point focuses on the concept of clarity and tranquility in the Tao — how a truly clear and tranquil state of mind can be reached, and how it can be maintained through responsive, skillful adjustments.

"True Tao" is a translation of the term *zhen dao* (真道). By using this term, Lao Tzu is implying that not all teachings are the same. All things in a category make sense relative to, and compared against, one another. When something is big, something else must be small. When someone is tall, someone else must be short. Therefore, the presence of teachings that are true, enlightening and helpful means there must also be teachings that are false, erroneous and unhelpful.

Often, erroneous teachings sound like what people want to hear. For instance, some say there is nothing you need to do to improve yourself, since you are already perfect; some say there is no good or bad, right or wrong, since all distinctions are illusory. Such teachings cannot create positive results that last, but they may seem attractive, at least initially.

One such teaching claims it is possible to achieve spiritual understanding quickly, even instantly. This, too, is what people want to hear. As Lao Tzu says in *Tao Te Ching* chapter 53:

> *The great Tao is broad and plain*
> *But people like the side paths*

A side path appears to be a shortcut that can save time and reduce effort, but it is not the great Tao. Its appearance is deceiving, because it ultimately leads nowhere. Anyone who promises instant enlightenment without much work is leading others down the side path.

In this verse, Lao Tzu makes it clear that entering the true Tao is a gradual process. No matter how spiritually gifted, one cannot attain enlightenment like cooking instant noodles — just add hot water and the meal is ready in a few minutes. Real understanding requires real work, and that is why we use the word "cultivate." Cultivating the Tao is similar to cultivating a field. It is about making a commitment for a lifetime, not just attending a few seminars.

In Buddhism, attaining Buddhahood is also a gradual process. Although some Buddhists speak of becoming suddenly enlightened, that enlightenment is still the result of dedicated work over time. It is always the progressive study of dharma that builds the foundation for the spirit to awaken. The awakening itself may occur in an instant, but the process leading up to it unfolds gradually.

The potential for this awakening is known as "Buddha-nature," and it exists in everyone. We all have the possibility of becoming the Buddha one day — if we are willing to nurture the seed of wisdom, and give it the time it needs to sprout and grow.

Another noteworthy point in this verse has to do with

the attainment of the Tao itself. There is potential for misunderstanding here, because the Tao is not an object, so it is not something you can get your hands on. The word "attainment" is used in a spiritual rather than physical sense.

What does it mean to attain the Tao spiritually? Some may assume it has something to do with mystical powers, but it is actually about discerning the right direction for yourself. In this context, the word "Tao" refers to your journey through life. There are numerous possible paths you can take, but not all of them will lead you to places you want to go. It is no trivial task to choose wisely, because the right path may not be obvious at all. Thus, attaining the Tao really means receiving the guidance to help you make the best possible choice.

This is why Lao Tzu specifically says "nothing has been obtained" in reference to attainment of the Tao. The transmission of the Tao provides no material rewards, only a clear direction to the right path. If you follow the

清靜經

direction, you will be on your way to rediscover your true self, regain the natural wisdom you have forgotten, and return to the oneness of the Tao.

The Buddhist view on this concept speaks to the same truth from a different angle. You get nothing when you attain the Tao, because the Buddha-nature has always been part of you. You cannot create it or destroy it; you cannot add to it or subtract from it. You can only awaken its dormant potential. Thus, when Huineng, the Sixth Patriarch of Zen Buddhism, received the spiritual transmission from the Fifth Patriarch and became enlightened, he exclaimed:

> *How unexpected that self-nature*
> *is originally clear and pure in itself!*
>
> *How unexpected that self-nature*
> *is originally not born or extinguished!*
>
> *How unexpected that self-nature*
> *is originally complete and sufficient in itself!*

How unexpected that self-nature
is originally not moved or shaken!

How unexpected that self-nature
is able to produce all dharmas!

Huineng was amazed to discover that the true nature of his being already contained everything, and yet it was also clear and pure. He felt he was given the world, and yet there was nothing for him to hold. All that the Fifth Patriarch did was point out the truth, and be the catalyst of his awakening.

Huineng kept this lesson in mind as he taught the Zen tradition to his own disciples. After he passed away, his disciples went forth to study with different masters. There is a story about one of them, as below:

The disciple bowed to Xing Si, a well-known monk of the Zen tradition. He expressed his wish to further his learning under the master.

Xing Si asked the disciple: "Where are you from?"

The disciple replied: "I am from the monastery of Huineng, the Sixth Patriarch."

Xing Si nodded, for Huineng was highly regarded throughout ancient China. He then asked: "What did you gain in studying under the Sixth Patriarch?"

The disciple said: "I gained nothing, because I was not lacking anything before I went to the monastery."

This response intrigued Xing Si. He decided to pursue it further: "If that is the case, then why did you have to go to the monastery?"

The disciple said: "If I hadn't gone there, how would I know that I was not lacking anything?"

Huineng taught this disciple well. Whether one is involved with Taoism, Buddhism, or any other wisdom tradition, the same principle applies. When you elevate your understanding to the next level, you attain nothing except the realization of your self-nature — which is everything.

Why do sages call it "attaining the Tao" if there is nothing to attain? One reason is that the expression makes an abstract concept easier to grasp. People are used to dealing with everyday objects, but may have trouble comprehending the emptiness of great spiritual truths. Knowing this, sages choose their words with care, to facilitate comprehension.

Understanding of the above will lead you to the integration of clarity and tranquility into your life. This, in turn, will take you gradually into the Tao. As you immerse yourself in cultivation, you will naturally have more influence on others. As you become mindfully aware, you will naturally want to share that awareness with others.

This is what "transmit the sacred Tao" means. Just as the ancient sages have invited you to walk the path with them, now it is your turn to invite others to walk the path with you.

In doing so, you may find that there seems to be nothing

to transmit, and yet Tao transmission is the ultimate honor. There seems to be no cost, and yet the Tao is the priceless treasure. It is everything in existence, because the Tao encompasses all. It is everything one will ever need, because the Tao is complete and sufficient in itself.

This is why we speak of *sheng dao* (聖道) or "the sacred Tao" in the *Qingjing Jing*. The Tao may not be a deity, but it is definitely the sacred journey of our lives. When we look at it with tranquil mind and clear perceptions, we can see the Tao stands revealed... as nothing less than the essence of divinity itself.

Questions for Reflection

1. Are you ready to walk the path of the true Tao?

2. Are you ready to share the sacred Tao with others?

3. Do you feel there is clarity and tranquility in your cultivation?

上下

Chapter 9: Levels

Lao Jun says:

High-level individuals do not contend;
low-level individuals like to contend.

High virtue is not virtuous;
low virtue is attached to virtue.

Those who have attachments,
do not understand the Tao and virtue.

This verse is about the essence of attachment, following previous chapters on how attachments manifest in life. Specifically, we drill down to two aspects: attachments that lead to contention, and attachments to virtues.

The first notion is that high-level individuals are not contentious. This is very much in keeping with the peaceful nature of Tao philosophy. In chapter 22 of the *Tao Te Ching*, we see the following about sages:

> *Because they do not contend*
> *the world cannot contend with them*

This clarifies that in the Tao, non-contention results from the mindful decision to disengage. It is not the reactive stance of turning the other cheek; rather, it is the proactive choice of detaching from the need to mix it up with others in the first place.

Here, we should also note that we are talking about contention in a more general sense. It is not just about people clashing against one another, physically or otherwise. The Tao concept of contention also covers people comparing themselves against one another, and competing to see who can get ahead or have more — especially in terms of materialistic pursuits.

We can look around to see that most people are engaged in this broader kind of contention. In our society, we see them constantly pushing each other aside to get in front, and stepping on each other to climb higher. Along the way, tempers flare and conflicts ensue.

Tao cultivators are different. They know contention is a primary attachment that gets in the way of spiritual growth. Therefore, they refrain from engaging in the contentious kind of social competition. They can do quite well in life, and yet feel no need to compare themselves against anyone else.

The distinction between higher and lower levels is not a value judgement of intrinsic nature. All human beings, by applying the Tao and bettering themselves, can ascend from one level to the next. Someone at a low level today may be at a much higher level years from now. No one is intrinsically superior or inferior — we are all just going through phases.

At the lower level, contention seems to make sense. The world appears to have limited resources, so it must be a zero-sum game. Whenever someone wins, someone else has to lose. You are determined to make sure that loser won't be you, so you fight for what should rightfully be yours. If others try to invade your turf, they will find you ready to beat them back.

In this mindset, life is a rat race. Everyone is trying to get ahead, so you constantly compare yourself against others. It's all about survival of the fittest, so you scramble for recognition, position, and power. You demand respect and attack those who "dis" you. Insults, offenses, and slanders can never be forgiven. They can only be avenged.

People at this level often ask themselves: "What if others attack me first?" and "What if others assume I must be weak when I follow the peaceful path?" Their thinking is perpetually fixed on the assumption of external malevolence and ill will. They are driven by fear and see the world as being full of dangers. They can only feel safe by always being defensive.

If you take this contentious approach to life, you will encounter two problems. The first is that the constant state of alert is no way to live. The more you worry about protecting yourself or staying one step ahead, the less peace of mind there is in your life. The stress and anxiety will take their toll on you sooner or later. This is the very opposite of the Tao ideal to live life with effortless smoothness and joyous grace.

The second problem is that the world reflects your internal essence. If you harbor contention in your heart, before too long you will find yourself in contentious situations. Conflicts manifest precisely because you are attached to fears about the possible harm from others. Your defensiveness invites challenges, so if you are

清靜經

constantly defending against others, you tend to bring more conflicts into your life.

Everything we have discussed depicts contention and non-contention as a reflection of yin and yang. Higher and lower levels correspond to positive and negative energies in this context. Thus, knowing one side of the duality leads to greater understanding of the other side.

When the ancient sages contemplated the above, they also realized this was a principle that applied not just to peace and chaos in one's life, but also to virtues in general. Their insight can be stated this way: the higher one rises in any virtuous practice, the less one fixates on the virtue, thus making one truly virtuous.

This is exactly what chapter 38 of the *Tao Te Ching* says:

> *High virtue is not virtuous*
> *Therefore it has virtue*

In the above, "not virtuous" means being unconcerned about virtuous behavior. Having let go of attachments

清靜經

to virtues, Tao cultivators at this level have no need to constantly keep them in mind. They can be themselves, let their natural virtues surface spontaneously, without being forced in any way.

This state of mind brings peace with oneself as well as the world, and this ties back to the first part of this verse. When you have no desire to demonstrate your virtues, there is also no need to compare or compete. When you have nothing to prove to anyone, you live without the stress of contentious tension. It is absolutely liberating.

This peaceful tranquility is at the heart of *Qingjing Jing*, and it affects your perception in a powerfully positive way. Instead of seeing resources as finite and limited, you begin to understand that the Tao is an infinite, inexhaustible source. Why fight over anything, when there is more than one can possibly use? Why bother playing the zero-sum game, when the real game is about creating win-win situations for all?

Just as contention within is reflected by the external

world, the same is true for the peace in your heart. The less you guard against people, the more you receive warm greetings and friendly smiles. The more you have kind thoughts toward others, the less you find yourself dragged into arguments. You can change how the world treats you simply by managing your internal states.

Before reaching this level of high virtue, most of us must work through the level of low virtue. This is where we can become too concerned about virtuous behavior. Rather than to let everything flow naturally, we may strive to be good, force ourselves to be pious, and even keep track of scores. The heart may be in the right place — get closer to the Tao — but the actions can be overly contrived, and therefore unnatural.

This is what "low virtue is attached to virtue" means in the *Qingjing Jing*, and chapter 38 of the *Tao Te Ching* also describes it in a similar way:

> *Low virtue never loses virtue*
> *Therefore it has no virtue*

This applies not just to beginning Tao cultivators, but also to people who have never heard of the Tao. Those with low virtue are often worried about the opinions of others. They wish to be seen as possessing virtues, so they frequently bring up their virtuous achievements. If they have done something that can be shown in a positive light, they want to make sure everyone knows about it.

This is an area of common understanding between Tao philosophy and Buddhist teachings, so it becomes a natural intersection of the two traditions. In the Tao, Lao Tzu points out that low virtue has no real virtue. In the Buddhist perspective, there is a story drawn from history to make a similar point:

About 1,500 years ago, Emperor Wu of the Liang Dynasty ruled China. He was devoted to Buddhism, so much so that people called him the Bodhisattva Emperor. This was a nickname he embraced with pride.

One day, news reached him that Bodhidharma, the 28th

Patriarch of Buddhism, had traveled thousands of miles from India to China. He was overjoyed and immediately ordered a respectful invitation.

Bodhidharma came to the palace, and the very first thing the emperor wanted to talk about was the huge amount of work he had done for Buddhism. He said: "As you may already know, ever since I ascended to the throne, I have built hundreds of temples, published countless sutras, and supported numerous monks of the sangha. How much merit would you say I have accumulated?"

With this question, the emperor was expecting to receive some sort of praise. He thought that, in all likelihood, Bodhidharma had already seen much of his work since his arrival. He was certain Bodhidharma would be impressed, and thus look upon him with favor.

Bodhidharma replied: "No merit at all."

This shocked the emperor. He stammered: "Why no merit at all?"

Bodhidharma explained: "What you have created is positive karma in the material world. It is like the shadow following you. It looks like it is there, but in actuality, there is nothing."

This perplexed the emperor. How could all his temples and sutras be nothing? He asked: "What would be the real merit then?"

Bodhidharma said: "Pure and clear wisdom, emptiness in the self — such would be the nature of real merit. It is not something that can be pursued in the material world."

The emperor was stunned. The words of Bodhidharma rang true. They illuminated the extent of his ignorance — and showed he was still far from Buddhahood.

Bodhidharma's answer, "no merit at all," echoed Lao Tzu's description of "low virtue." Although the two of them lived centuries apart, they both looked at the world with the same clear perception.

This was the clarity that revealed the difference in virtuous works. What the emperor had provided was the virtue of prosperity, or *fu de* (福德). It was externally directed to material resources. Its very nature meant it must always be tied to the transience of the material world.

What the Bodhidharma practiced and taught was the virtue of merit, or *gong de* (功德). As the complement of *fu de*, it was internally directed to the realization of the true self. Bodhidharma described it as "pure and clear wisdom," which happened to match the theme of the *Qingjing Jing*.

Bodhidharma knew the emperor did not understand the above. If one accomplished good deeds externally, while harboring thoughts of superiority and personal glory internally, then there could be no merit at all. This would always be the case, regardless of the number of good deeds done.

The emperor assumed that the virtue of prosperity he accumulated was the same as the virtue of merit. Bodhidharma informed him it was quite the opposite:

none of work he did in the material world translated to the spiritual realm. If the emperor wished to accumulate true merit, the only way to do that would be to look within and focus on spirituality.

Bodhidharma did not minimize what the emperor had accomplished, because the virtue of prosperity was not negative, only incomplete. It was like one half of the yin and yang symbol. It needed the other half — the virtue of merit — to attain balanced oneness. This meant the emperor's effort in support of Buddhism could be truly virtuous, but only if it flowed from pure compassion, and was done for the sake of goodness rather than recognition.

The emperor not only desired recognition, he also felt *deserving* of it. He had become accustomed to praise, particular from those who called him "Bodhisattva Emperor." This was why he thought he could claim credit with the Bodhidharma. He grasped onto his works with attachment — and so became the classic

清靜經

example of low virtue, as defined by both the *Tao Te Ching* and the *Qingjing Jing*.

Without the shock from Bodhidharma's words, the emperor would still be stuck at low virtue. He might aspire to high virtue, but his expectation of external approval proved he was not there yet. As long as he held on to this attachment, he could not be a bodhisattva — a being of wisdom and compassion only one step away from Buddhahood.

The same is true for all of us. We, too, can be stuck at low virtue if we continue holding on to our own attachments. We may cling to the good deeds we have done, the people we have helped, or the effort we have expended on their behalf. If so, this would indicate incomplete understanding of the Tao and virtue, exactly as the *Qingjing Jing* says.

In order to transition from low to high, we must know the difference between them. High virtue is uncommon, like artistic perfection. It already says everything that should be said, so there is no need to say anything more. Low virtue is common, like consumer products. It needs a massive marketing campaign, because that is the only way to boost its perceived value.

In chapter 41 of the *Tao Te Ching*, Lao Tzu describes the difference between the levels this way:

> *Higher people hear of the Tao*
> *They diligently practice it*
> *Average people hear of the Tao*
> *They sometimes keep it and sometimes lose it*
> *Lower people hear of the Tao*
> *They laugh loudly at it*

Higher-level people practice the Tao diligently, because they are free of attachments. They can look through the surface appearance of the world to see the underlying reality, so to them practicing the Tao is essential to life. Their focus is inward, to seek answers within the heart. They follow the Tao with serious intent, because their diligence comes naturally.

Lower-level people laugh at the Tao loudly, because they are still mired in attachments. They see only the surface appearance, so to them practicing the Tao seems like a waste of time that brings no material benefits. Their focus is outward, in chasing one distraction after another. They sneer at the Tao, because they are not aware of their own misunderstanding.

By using the above as a guide, you can gauge your progress as you work your way up in spirituality. As you improve yourself, you will become more consistent in your practice. Harmful attachments will lose strength and disappear. Over time, you will find it less and less necessary to remind yourself about the virtues, as they become integrated into your being.

The result of the above is your continuing personal transformation. You may have started out at a lower level, but now you can feel the Tao lifting you to the higher level of peace, harmony, and non-contention. You may have started out with low virtue, but now you can see the path elevating you to the higher mindset, where virtues flow naturally and effortlessly.

Your affinity to the Tao grows with every step on this path — and ultimately, this will be the best preparation you can make in facing the challenges of life.

清靜經

Questions for Reflection

1. Do you need to remind yourself to refrain from contention?

2. Do you need to remind yourself to practice virtues?

3. Do you feel a need for validation or praise from others?

146

妄心

Chapter 10: Deluded Minds

*The reason why sentient beings are unable to attain the
true Tao, is because they have deluded minds.*

*Since they have deluded minds,
they startle the spirit.*

*Since the spirit is startled,
they become attached to myriad things.*

*Since they are attached to myriad things,
they form covetous thoughts.*

*Since they form covetous thoughts,
they become anxious.*

The mind can be a double-edged sword. When it is free of delusions, it can be the most powerful tool for one's cultivation; when it is saddled with delusions, it can be the greatest obstacle in one's path.

One of the common delusions people have is about material things. We all need a certain amount to survive in the world, so there is nothing intrinsically wrong with the material things themselves. The delusion only comes about when we forget the greater purpose of life, and let material things become that purpose.

Some fall into this trap because they are too busy making a living. They rarely pause to think about why they do what they do. They become narrowly focused on narrow goals — earning a certain amount of money, taking a particular position of power, and so on. Each level of materialistic achievement opens up additional possibilities to achieve even more.

As the prominence of these achievements increases, so too do the fears associated with them. What if the money, the position and the status are still not enough? What if they are obtained, only to be lost? What if they are taken away, by force or trickery?

It's not just inadequacy or loss. Some may fear even more the loss of face — their carefully crafted image, public perception and reputation. What if that is lost too? What will people think? What will people say?

This is exactly what Lao Tzu expresses in chapter 13 of the *Tao Te Ching*:

> *Favor and disgrace make one fearful*
> *The greatest misfortune is the self*

Although people tend to think of favor as good and disgrace as bad, in reality they can both lead to startling fears. Although the spirit prefers the clear and tranquil, one can be so disturbed that clarity and tranquility become impossible. In trying to do something about this imbalance, the mind grasps at straws, and forms even more attachments.

This downward spiral can become a vicious circle. The more one is attached to things, the more one will covet. Obtaining a coveted object will not necessarily satisfy the attachment. Indeed, it can make things worse. This is the central theme in the following story:

Once upon a time in ancient China, there was a farmer who lived in poverty. He always thought he would remain poor his entire life — until one day, when he made an unexpected discovery.

He was tilling his field when he struck something solid. He thought it was a large rock, so he tried to dig it out. When he removed more of the dirt around it, he realized it was a statue. He pulled it out carefully, and saw that it was some sort of Buddhist figure. Thinking he might have stumbled upon treasures, the farmer dug around in that general area, but found nothing more.

He cleaned up his find and took it to an antique expert to get it appraised. The expert was stunned to see it. "Incredible!" he exclaimed. "This is a genuine Arhat of the Mahayana. It has been missing for centuries!"

The farmer did not understand any of this, so the antique expert explained: "In the Mahayana tradition of Buddhism, the original followers of the Buddha are greatly revered. Each one of them is said to be an Arhat, a perfect being far along the path of enlightenment. All of them together are known as the Eighteen Arhats. Long ago, statues of them were created as a complete set, but they were all lost in the last great war. Congratulations! You have found one of them, and it is extremely valuable."

He told the farmer exactly how valuable it was, and the farmer could hardly believe it. In that moment, he knew he would never have to till his fields again. He and his family were set for life.

He went home to give his wife the good news. His wife was excited at first, but then became puzzled when she saw the deep frown on his face. "What's wrong?" she asked. "We now have more wealth than we ever dreamed. Why do you look so anxious?"

"How can I not be anxious?" The farmer said as he hurried to leave the house. "There are seventeen more statues like it out there somewhere. I must get back to digging so I can find them all!"

We can see from the above that the mental process of the farmer was exactly as described in this part of the *Qingjing Jing*: the farmer's spirit was startled by his find, and he became attached to it. This attachment gave rise to covetous thoughts, which in turn made him anxious.

When one is caught in this trap, one is fixated on an obsession to the exclusion of everything else. The mind has been deluded, so the afflicted individual keeps going. Sooner or later, the damage to life becomes too great to ignore. Family, friends and loved ones are neglected. Exhaustion sets in, and one loses the ability to enjoy anything, great or small.

Many who pursue wealth do not realize that an amassed fortune generates its own needs and requires attention. They may think they are masters of their possessions, but they become slaves instead. Stress, tension, and worries dominate their lives. This is the beginning of the end. Soon, everything falls apart.

The above is how people descend into suffering, step by step. Delusions take them far from the Tao, and only clarity and tranquility can bring them back. This is in complete agreement with chapter 3 of the *Tao Te Ching*, where we see the following:

> *Do not treasure goods that are hard to obtain*
> *So the people will not become thieves*
> *Do not show the desired things*
> *So their hearts will not be confused*

The "goods that are hard to obtain" in this passage point to the myriad things that we become attached to in the *Qingjing Jing*. Think of sports cars that draw envious stares on the road, or the latest gadgets that attract long lines of people eagerly waiting to make their purchase.

One certainly cannot deny that such objects exert a

清靜經

powerful pull. There are so many temptations out there, and they are like strong winds that sweep people off their feet — a force that most cannot resist.

Moreover, our attachments in this world include not just material things, but also the intangible aspects of life. Obsessive behaviors may not center around objects at all. Rather, they may be related to emotions and events.

At the individual level, people may harbor memories of past failures and personal regrets that they dwell on. They become attached to "if only" thoughts — if only I had done this and not that; if only I had said this instead of that. Some are haunted by such thoughts all their lives, thus missing out on any possibility of lasting happiness.

In personal relationships, people may be so attached to loved ones that they turn a positive relationship into a negative dependency. This can be especially damaging for those who tie their mental well-being to someone else's actions beyond their control. They are often unwilling to detach themselves, thus perpetuating and worsening the problem.

In disputes from social interactions, people may hold a grudge for years, even decades. They find it impossible to forgive someone for certain words or deeds. This creates bitter resentment that can be extremely toxic, leading to deluded mind and startled spirit. Some embark on a path of revenge, leading to even more drastic and tragic outcomes.

All these examples and more manifest as emotional storms. They are usually driven by the fear of loss — anything from the loss of status or reputation to the loss of friends and family. This fear can be overwhelming, even crippling, and the suffering can be extremely painful, even before the loss actually occurs.

For many of us, such storms are a frequent occurrence. They come one after another and never seem to stop. We may still be dealing with one particular temptation and all the problems that come with it, when something else hits us out of nowhere. Life seems like a never-ending parade of things to worry about, giving us no break and no rest.

The best protection from the above is the Tao. The sages teach that all our attachments to the myriad things — tangible or intangible, past or future — are sourced in the material world, and therefore have no lasting reality. The trends people obsess over this year become old news next year; the grievances people hold on to all their lives become meaningless on the deathbed. This is a realization that shields us from emotional storms, as if we have sailed into a safe harbor when the seas become turbulent.

The *Qingjing Jing* goes even further to pinpoint the root cause of suffering. Anxieties are the result of covetous thoughts, which come from attachments formed by the spirit that was startled by the deluded mind. Thus, delusions are at the very beginning of the chain reaction.

They are the first domino that causes all others to fall one by one.

The way to address delusions is to restore tranquility and right the mind. If we can do that, then the chain reaction never starts, the dominoes remain standing, and whatever problems we had before fade away. The winds of temptation are still there, and for most people they are still too strong to resist — but for us they are more like a soft breeze.

Indeed, we can venture out into the raging storms of the world in perfect safety. Delusions, attachments, and covetous thoughts have all lost their power over us. Protected by Tao wisdom and Buddhist teachings, we can continue on our journey with confidence, security… and the greatest ease.

清靜經

Questions for Reflection

1. Are there material things to which you are especially attached?

2. Are you sometimes tempted by covetous thoughts?

3. Have you ever wanted something so much that it made you anxious?

Chapter 11: Suffering

Afflicted with anxieties and delusions,
worrying and suffering in body and mind,

often encountering murkiness and disgrace,
drifting aimlessly in birth and death,

constantly immersed in the ocean of bitterness,
forever losing the true Tao.

Of all the lessons taught by the Buddha, the first and foremost was suffering. The Sanskrit term used by the Buddha was *dukkha*, which denoted negativity in life that could range from a vague feeling of unease all the way to unbearable pain and devastating despair. This term is translated to the Chinese character *ku* (苦), meaning bitterness. It had become widely known and understood by the time of the *Qingjing Jing*.

As we move through life, we all experience ups and downs. Sometimes things turn out well; other times, not so well. When we look at the low points, we can see the failure and frustration as part of the *ku* in life. Think about all the times we experience suffering, such as:

- When we have desires, but cannot fulfill them no matter what we do.
- When we have loved ones, but cannot be with them, or must be separated from them.
- When we have people, things or events that we dislike, but cannot avoid no matter what we do or which way we go.

清靜經

The above factors and more lead to unhappy moments. In those moments, we feel heartache and hopelessness, depression and despair — and such negative emotions are a form of suffering in themselves.

Suffering is linked to every stage of life. This is often expressed as *sheng lao bing si* (生老病死) in Mandarin. It means all living things must go through the physical and mental suffering associated with birth, aging, sickness and death.

No one is exempt. We may not remember the pain of being born, but we all know the misery of being sick. We may feel like immortals while we are young, but before too long we start to feel the weakening effects of age. As the years go by, the body and mind slow down and become less functional. This cannot be stopped; it will continue to torment us until we die.

What about life? What about the victories we can achieve? What about joy and happiness? Do these not offset death, setbacks and heartbreaks?

The good things in life are part of *dukkha* as well. Impermanence is the hallmark of our existence, so whatever bliss we experience will not last indefinitely. Every moment of enjoyment or triumph will come to an end. Even a lifetime blessed with a happy marriage will eventually end in the death of the beloved or oneself. In this perspective, positive experiences of life do not balance out the negative. Rather, they accentuate the suffering — the happier you are when you have something good, the more painful it will be when you lose it.

In Buddhist teachings, everything above characterizes the cycle of birth, death and rebirth known as *Samsara*. Sentient beings are caught in it, repeatedly experiencing *dukkha* as they stumble from life to death and back again.

The above seems rather bleak, and perhaps that is why Buddhism has often been diluted and distorted in the West. Instead of talking about the inevitability of suffering, teachers tend to expand upon the attainment of peace and a blissful state of mind. The overall effect seems to be the maximizing of optimism, and the minimizing of pessimism.

The Buddha did not consider his perspective to be pessimistic. He only wished to describe existence accurately, to view life in a way that was as realistic as possible. This was neither optimism nor pessimism; it was simply a coherent collection of facts that could not be refuted.

Moreover, the Buddha did not just state the problem. He also described the solution in depth and detail. One can take heart in the realization that there is a real possibility for liberation from suffering, and there is a clearly defined path leading to it. Thus, the picture painted by the Buddha was not bleak. He emphasized that there was a ray of hope, and the solution was available to everyone.

The Buddha summarized these ideas and taught the Four Noble Truths, as follows:

清靜經

1. *Dukkha* — the reality of suffering or dissatisfaction that sentient beings cannot avoid.

2. *Samudaya* — the origin of *dukkha* is the craving or attachments that we all experience.

3. *Nirodha* — the cessation of *dukkha* is possible for everyone through the elimination of attachments.

4. *Magga* — the way to the cessation of suffering is the Eightfold Path.

These four spiritual truths are further explained with a story told by the Buddha, as recorded in the *Lotus Sutra*:

Once upon a time, there lived an elder who possessed great wealth and a large mansion in a village. This mansion had one gate in front, and was very old. It was starting to show its age, with crumbling walls and cracks appearing in places. Nevertheless, it was home to his family, including many children.

One day, something caught on fire in the mansion. The fire quickly blazed out of control in all directions, and would soon consume the entire mansion. When the elder saw this, he thought: "I can escape the mansion safely, but the children are still inside. They are unaware of the danger, and they have no idea they need to escape. I must save them!"

He went into the mansion and found the children engrossed in play. He told them about the fire, and tried to gather them together so they could get out immediately. He knew there was only one path out of the mansion, so in order to escape the fire, they needed to move quickly.

The children were not alarmed. They did not know what fire was, and they had no concept of danger, loss, or the necessity to get out of the mansion. They all chose to ignore his words and disregard his warning. They went back to playing their games.

The situation was getting desperate. What to do? The elder decided he had to try a different approach. If he could not force them out or carry them out, then perhaps he could think of a way to lure them out.

He called to the children and told them there were three carts outside the mansion that he had prepared for them. Each cart was pulled by a different kind of animal: goats, deer, or oxen. They were the rare kind of toys that the elder knew the children liked.

As he expected, the ploy worked. The children rushed out of the mansion to see the carts for themselves. Once they were outside, well away from danger, the elder felt much relieved.

The children looked around, but did not see the carts as promised, so they asked the elder: "Where are the carts pulled by goats, deer and oxen?"

The elder presented to them something even better: a large carriage, decorated with jewels, staffed by many servants, and pulled by a giant white ox.

The children were delighted. They quickly climbed into the magnificent carriage. Along with the elder, they set off for a distant destination, far away from the burning mansion.

In this story, the elder represents an awakened soul like

清靜經

the Buddha, someone who has become aware of the situation facing mankind. The mansion is the material plane of existence. The fire burning the mansion is the problem of human suffering that is consuming our world, even as we speak.

We are the children playing with one another in the mansion. We are completely engrossed in our games — fame and fortune, power and prestige, competition and contention.

Perhaps, at some point in the past, there were wise teachers who told us we had neglected the spiritual side of life. We are not too sure about that — because we didn't pay attention, just like the children ignoring the elder in the story.

The carts pulled by goats, deer and oxen are the entry-level teachings of Buddhism. When we encounter these teachings for the first time, we are like the children lured outside the mansion. If we study Buddhist thoughts and go beyond the entry level, we become like the children seeing the great carriage of the magnificent white ox. This carriage is the advanced teachings of the Buddha, and its distant destination is the cessation of suffering.

This verse from the *Qingjing Jing* explores the same topic from a different perspective, using a different metaphor. Instead of the burning mansion, the existence of *dukkha* is *ku hai* (苦海), the ocean of bitterness. This ocean extends indefinitely in all directions, just like human suffering is pervasive in all aspects of life.

The *Qingjing Jing* describes all sentient beings as "constantly immersed in the ocean of bitterness." This is because we cannot help but be subject to all the challenges of life, simply by virtue of being alive.

This is something that applies to all, not just to the unaware. Many worldly people can be quite adept at creating delusions for themselves. They think they can solve their own problems if they learn yet another technique or read yet another self-help book. Invariably, the new technique or book proves to be ineffective. They shrug it off and move on to learn the next technique and read the next book, while still immersed in *ku hai*.

I know someone who fits the above description. He deals with the issues in his life by reading numerous books, some of them several times. They have given him new ways to complain about his problems, while doing absolutely nothing to solve them.

He has trapped himself with his own intelligence. He is so attached to knowledge that absorbing new ideas is more important than actually using them. He delves into many theories — and that's all he ever does. Who has the time to do anything in actual practice when there are so many more fascinating books to read? He does not realize that the books for him are like the toys for the children in the burning mansion. As long as he remains engrossed in them, he will be, as the *Qingjing Jing* says, "forever losing the true Tao."

In the Buddha's story, the elder lured the children outside with the promise of novelty. In the Tao, the sages hope to awaken us by pointing to the problems in our existence. Think about the anxieties that saturate your life, all the physical and mental suffering you have tolerated until now. None of it is how things ought to be. Deep down, you know there has to be a better way.

That better way, like the carriage of the white ox, is what will finally take us away from *dukkha*. In the paradigm of *ku hai*, it is a boat that can sail through the ocean of bitterness.

Suffering is a part of life, so the ocean of bitterness will always exist. There is no denying its reality, but we don't have to remain immersed in it. The message from the *Qingjing Jing* is that the situation is not at all hopeless.

Like the children climbing into the carriage in the story, we can get out of the ocean and climb aboard the boat. Just as the carriage is the Buddha's vehicle to take its passengers to the cessation of suffering, the boat is the vessel that will take us to the oneness of the Tao. Why should we float around, treading water and getting nowhere, when we can sail the ocean with ease and comfort?

The *Qingjing Jing* is the boat that has come to your rescue. With you onboard, we are now ready to resume our journey. We have charted a course that will take us where we want to go. We expect there will be rough weather ahead, but we will sail through the stormy seas together. Sooner or later, this boat will arrive at our destination: the other shore, the shore of enlightenment.

Questions for Reflection

1. Have you ever felt lost and adrift in life?

2. Have you ever searched for the meaning of life?

3. Have you ever experienced anxieties that caused suffering in body, mind and spirit?

清靜

Chapter 12: Clarity and Tranquility

The Tao that is true and constant:
those who realize it will attain it by themselves;

those who realize and attain the Tao,
will possess constant clarity and tranquility!

In the final verse of the *Qingjing Jing*, we come full circle back to the concepts of clarity and tranquility. They are the true Tao because they represent a genuine path to solve the problem of human suffering. They are the constant Tao because the path has always been there, and will always be there for us. It is often said that when the student is ready, the master appears. Here, we can say when the traveler is ready, the path appears.

In this verse, Lao Tzu says "those who realize it will attain it by themselves," meaning it is up to you to understand the Tao on your own. Reading the words of others is not enough, nor is following a particular teacher. The best teacher in the world cannot cultivate for you, just as you cannot cultivate for anyone else. The Tao that you experience firsthand is something that becomes uniquely yours. It is of no use or value to others, but infinitely useful and valuable to you.

It is like drinking water. When you are thirsty, you have no choice but to slake your thirst. Others can slake their own thirst, but never yours. Once the water is in you, it becomes part of you. It benefits you and no one else. If you wish to share its benefits with others, the most you can do is lead them to the water. It will then be up to them to drink on their own.

Beware of self-proclaimed masters who promise to cleanse your negative karma or magically accelerate your cultivation. What they offer is no different from having someone eat your food, and somehow filling your stomach — that is simply not how it works.

As we near the end of final verse, Lao Tzu speaks of "those who realize and attain the Tao." Who are they? Who among us can master this attainment, to be one with clarity and tranquility?

The answer is everyone. Everyone has the Tao within, just as everyone has Buddha-nature within. You don't need a fancy title or an academic degree. You only need the willingness to engage in a sustained practice of authentic teachings. You don't need to be anyone special or possess any special knowledge. Your true self is already complete and sufficient for the realization and attainment of the Tao.

In the *Qingjing Jing*, that journey takes the form of a voyage — the boat taking you through the ocean of bitterness, as described in the previous chapter. Thus, when providing spiritual assistance, Chinese cultivators often speak of *du ren* (渡人), meaning to ferry people. This may be cryptic to someone who has never heard of the sailing metaphor, but should now make a lot of sense.

To ferry people in this context means helping others by lifting them out of the ocean of bitterness so they can sail with you. This imagery is frequently used in Buddhism. The *Heart Sutra*, for example, ends with a mantra that celebrates everyone reaching the other shore together — the shore of enlightenment that we can call the Tao.

Many of us still need to cultivate a lot more just to be a little wiser. That means the other shore is still far off, well beyond visual range. If we cannot see it, then how will we know which way to go? How can we tell which direction to sail?

With the *Qingjing Jing*, the message from Lao Tzu is that we should use constant clarity and tranquility as our map and compass. If we follow their guidance, we will see land appearing on the horizon before too long.

With constant clarity, you look through the material world in order to discern its illusions. You look through human nature in order to distinguish truths from lies. You look through existence in order to perceive the source of creation and the cycles of nature. Reality itself becomes like an open book to you.

With constant tranquility, you possess a profound calmness within that cannot be disrupted by chaos. Although the world can still be crazy at times, it does not get to you. No matter how noisy it may be externally, you remain at peace internally. Together with constant clarity, your inner peace elevates you to a whole new level of being.

Constant clarity and tranquility are the highest level of oneness with the Tao. That oneness is what Lao Tzu refers to in chapter 22 of the *Tao Te Ching*:

> *Therefore the sages hold to the one*
> *as an example for the world*

The one initiates all and enables everything that follows. The one is connected to your true self, which already has everything you need to accomplish anything you want. Thus, to hold to the one is to embrace constant clarity and tranquility.

Lao Tzu drives home this point in chapter 39 of the *Tao Te Ching*:

> *The sky attained oneness and thus clarity*
> *The earth attained oneness and thus tranquility*

When these lines are applied to the personal level, they illuminate both the *Tao Te Ching* and the *Qingjing Jing*. These classics are not about abstract philosophies. Rather, they are about you. Ultimately, you are the one who must attain the oneness of the Tao through clarity and tranquility. Then, the Tao becomes the source of lasting clarity and tranquility in your world.

You might have thought of yourself as one of the people rescued by the vessel sailing through the ocean of bitterness. Now, you can see there is more to it than that. You are actually the owner of the vessel as well. Nothing happens without you.

Just as clarity and tranquility are one in the Tao, the many roles onboard the vessel are one in you. You are no longer the passenger, without any duties. It is your responsibility to command and navigate. You are in charge.

As we near the end of the *Qingjing Jing*, you have completed the first part of your journey — constant clarity and constant tranquility. You have arrived at a port of call, but there is still a long way to go. After a brief respite, you must set sail again, for the final destination.

You will not travel alone. More and more students of the Tao have become aware of the *Qingjing Jing*, and that means fellow travelers will join you for the next leg of the journey.

You are ready for departure. You feel confident, because you will be guided by the wisdom of Lao Tzu and the Buddha. May you enjoy fair winds and calm seas ahead in your continuing voyage. Smooth sailing!

清靜經

Questions for Reflection

1. Do you realize that clarity and tranquility are your original nature?

2. Do you realize that you can attain clarity and tranquility on your own?

3. Do you realize that you must now, in your own way, help convey the same realization to others?

About the Author

Derek Lin is the award-winning author of popular books in the Tao genre: *The Tao of Daily Life, The Tao of Success, The Tao of Joy Every Day, The Tao of Happiness,* and *The Tao of Wisdom*. He has also utilized his linguistic skills to create *Tao Te Ching: Annotated & Explained*, a translation lauded by critics as setting a new standard for accuracy, and faithfully capturing the lyrical beauty of the original.

He was born in Taiwan and grew up with native fluency in both Chinese and English. This background enables him to convey Eastern teachings to Western readers in a way that is clear, simple, and authentic. He is an active speaker and educator on the *Tao Te Ching* and Tao philosophy.

www.DerekLin.com

THE TAO OF DAILY LIFE

The Mysteries of the Orient Revealed

The Joys of Harmony Found

The Path to Enlightenment Illuminated

The Tao of Daily Life combines ancient Eastern wisdom with practical application in a way that is perfect for modern Western readers. Derek Lin, expert in Eastern philosophy, brings this time-honored Chinese spiritual thought system into the twenty-first century.

"There is one simple reason for the Tao to have survived through the ages intact: it works," writes Lin. "The principles of the Tao are extremely effective when applied to life. The philosophy as a whole is nothing less than a practical, useful guide to living life in a way that is smooth, peaceful, and full of energy."

THE TAO OF SUCCESS

The Five Ancient Rings of Destiny

This is a journey of self-exploration, starting from your innermost spiritual core and expanding outward to your mind, your relationships, your world, and ultimately your destiny.

The ancients defined success not in terms of material wealth but in terms of becoming the best version of yourself in every possible way. This is the map that will show you how to get there.

THE TAO OF JOY EVERY DAY

365 Days of Tao Living

This is a yearlong journey, traveling at the speed of one page per day. That one page may not seem like much, but it can set the tone for the entire day, so you can be immersed in the Tao as you go through it.

Over time, this practice transforms you gradually into a Tao-centric individual. It is the easiest way to cultivate spirituality for those who simply can't find the time for such pursuits.

THE TAO OF HAPPINESS

Stories from Chuang Tzu for Your Spiritual Journey

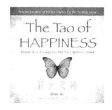

If you have not encountered Chuang Tzu before, prepare yourself for a treat. He was the sage who stood apart from all others in Chinese history. He was a unique presence, a great mind like no one before or since.

Chuang Tzu quickly distinguished himself and became well known for his deep understanding and sense of humor. His mastery was such that he could explain the Tao with simple stories, and his humor was such that he could see the joy in ordinary things. He taught his students about "carefree wandering" — the path of moving through life with a free and happy heart, regardless of how turbulent the journey might be.

THE TAO OF WISDOM

Ancient Stories Bringing the Tao Te Ching to Life

The Tao of Wisdom is the book for anyone who is interested in the *Tao Te Ching* and wants to understand it more deeply. With this book, Derek Lin brings you inspirational stories that reveal the profound meaning of key passages and central concepts in the Tao. The wise words of Lao Tzu come into clear focus like never before.

This book is Derek Lin's return to the format of his award-winning and bestselling *The Tao of Daily Life*. Once again, he combines his knowledge of ancient texts and storytelling skills in another masterwork — an excellent guide for learning Eastern philosophy in the Western world.

TAO TE CHING

Annotated & Explained

The enduring wisdom of the *Tao Te Ching* can become a companion for your own spiritual journey.

Reportedly written by a sage named Lao Tzu over 2,500 years ago, the *Tao Te Ching* is one of the most succinct — and yet among the most profound — spiritual texts ever written. Short enough to read in an afternoon, subtle enough to study for a lifetime, the *Tao Te Ching* distills into razor-sharp poetry centuries of spiritual inquiry into the Tao — the "Way" of the natural world around us that reveals the ultimate organizing principle of the universe.

Printed in Great Britain
by Amazon

48119173R00118